# Here Be Dragons

This edition published in 2008 by Natula Publications
Natula Ltd., 5 St Margarets Avenue, Christchurch, Dorset BH23 1JD

ISBN 9781897887721

A CIP catalogue record of this book is available from the British Library.

Printed by Cpod, Trowbridge, Wiltshire.

Illustration on Page 41 reproduced from *The Cerne Giant*
by kind permission of Rodney Castleton.

Illustrations on Pages 37, 53 ,54 and back cover
by kind permission of Eric Cockain.

Front cover illustration: Wessex Wyvern.

Back cover illustrations: Carvings from Christchurch Priory Church.
Top: Dragon elbow rest in the Great Quire.
Middle: Green Man in the Cloister Way.
Bottom: Harpy in the Great Quire.

# Contents

# Dedication

This book is respectfully dedicated to my friend
Dr. Alistair F. Somerville Ford,
philanthropist.
Chairman, The Institute of Commercial Management,
The Fusée, Bargates, Christchurch, Dorset.

# Introduction

*Here Be Dragons* examines the history of dragons, the different types and the cultural differences, while trying to determine the idea of what is a dragon in different times and places.

The book relates stories of saints battling with dragons and deals with English folklore about them, concentrating on Wessex in particular, and especially the Christchurch area. There are many dragon carvings in Christchurch Priory.

Ley lines, which can also be known as 'dragon lines', as dragons are supposed to fly in straight lines, are straight line alignments which pass over ancient sites and horizon features. This book also identifies some local ley lines and these are shown in full in the appendices. Ley lines probably originated as Neolithic farming calendars and remained in use for generations. Such alignments exist all over Great Britain and overseas, wherever the first farmers needed calendars at a time before people could read and write.

# What were dragons?

Dragons are one of the oldest of the mythical creatures and occur in the oral and written traditions of almost every civilisation, dating back thousands of years. Legend has dragons living at the bottom of the sea, in the sky, deep underground in the centre of the earth, in caves or on hilltops. Usually they have wings, claws, a long tail, and scales on their bodies; they breathe fire and guard vast hoards of treasure. They are often made up of different animal parts and may sometimes have more than one head. In some cases, they are even able to change their shape and colour.

The dragon appears to be based on the idea of a flying crocodile able to breathe fire, hence a mixture of fact and myth.

The crocodile is real and the dragon story appears to have two origins: a military title or banner in the Roman Empire and fabulous tales based on sailors' stories about large salt-water crocodiles found at the mouths of equatorial rivers. Ancient maps often bore the legend 'Here Be Dragons' at these river estuaries such as in West Africa.

There is no set definition of a dragon and they take on different forms and are awarded various attributes depending on the culture. However, there is a considerable difference between the dragons of western cultures and those of the east, not only in their anatomy but also in their behaviour, their symbolism and their effect on their particular culture.

The eastern dragon is held in high esteem and valued for its majesty and magical powers. It is seen as a protector and a symbol of beauty and power. The Chinese dragon lives in the sky, has horns and represents fertility and wisdom. The Chinese 'year of the dragon' (which occurs every 12 years) is said to be a very prosperous year for the people of China and people born in the 'year of the dragon' are deemed to be healthy, wealthy and wise, all attributes that the dragon of the east represents.

**Chinese Dragon**

The western dragon, however, is viewed as a terrifying villain and is usually thought to be venomous, cruel, cunning, bloodthirsty and evil. Western dragons are known for terrorising communities and sometimes for eating humans, particularly children. Most western dragon legends are concerned with protecting the community or a person, such as a princess or maiden in distress, from it by slaying or taming the troublesome dragon. In Britain, anyone who killed a dragon seemed to be a knight or was awarded a knighthood as a result. Dragon legends in the west refer to sea dragons (monsters), which can be of great size and length, or of dragons which live in the earth, in caves, wells, lakes and roots of the World Tree.

The dragon's image has been found in cave paintings and painted on rocks in China thousands of years before the birth of Christ. The ancient Egyptians worshipped dragons, too, the cult gradually spread throughout the Orient and eastwards reaching its peak during the days of the Roman Empire. Dragons were supposed to have very good eyesight and to be able to foretell the future.

Christianity identified dragons with the devil; the serpent being a form of dragon, hence we have a dragon in the Garden of Eden.

Early dragon stories have the creature living in water like a crocodile and only becoming associated with fire later. Marco Polo apparently said that he had discovered dragons when he spotted crocodiles during his travels to China in 13th century. Fabulous tales based on sailors' stories of these large crocodiles or other strange sea monsters encountered in their travels may well have given rise to legends about dragons. Images of dragons could have arrived in Britain as early as the Bronze Age with Phoenician tin traders. The fire-breathing dragon is probably based on the poison-spitting cobra of India.

The wording 'here be dragons' could be found on ancient maps where the compiler did not know how to record unexplored territory and also at the edges of maps. When the world was still considered to be flat, these dragons were thought to be at the edge of the earth waiting to eat anyone who was foolish enough to sail too close.

The concept of dragons flying may have come with the silk trade from China, where dragons are the national symbol and were seen as somewhat friendly creatures. Although usually without wings, Chinese dragons lived in the sky and gave spiritual enlightenment. The constellation of Draco (dragon) held the pole star Thuban at about 3000 B.C. and the meteorites known as Draconids appear from there. In late medieval times, stuffed lizards had bat wings stuck on to them and were sold as preserved baby dragons.

In ancient Rome, dragons were thought to hold the mysteries of the earth. The Romans looked to them as a source of knowledge and strength. The Roman military used two forms of dragon: one for heroism to protect them and the other, a fierce dragon to frighten the enemy. The dragon banner was made to operate like a windsock so that air passing through it gave it shape. The dragon was the badge of a cohort, a military unit rather like an infantry battalion, able to operate as an independent body. The cohort's standard bearer was a draconarius. (The badge of a legion was an eagle.) The Romans borrowed their military dragon from enemies they met in their Eastern Empire. When the

Roman Empire divided between Rome and Constantinople, the Eastern Emperor adopted the dragon banner.

Dragons are often associated with hill forts, perhaps a reminder of military traditions and of former battles between Romans and Britons or between Britons and Saxons. Throughout the Wessex region (Wessex was Hampshire, Dorset, Somerset, Wiltshire, southern Gloucestershire and western Berkshire) there are many earthworks and hill forts showing that this area was thriving and well-populated before the Romans invaded it. Military units from these counties often included dragons in their cap badge up to current times.

**Flying Serpent Dragon**
**A combination of Dragon as bringer of Death**
**and Serpent as representation of Wisdom**

The 2nd Augusta Legion, which conquered south and south-west Britain after 43 A.D., had a Capricorn as its badge. This mythological beast was the front-half (head, horns and forelegs) of a goat and the back half and tail of a cuttlefish. The Capricorn may have given rise to the Wessex Wyvern (a dragon with only two legs).

The Roman usage of the dragon was maintained in Britain after the last legion left in 407 A.D., withdrawn to help defend closer to home. The British war leader of the Britons' own field army based on the Roman dux bellorum, duke of battles, was Arthur, perhaps the son of Uther Pendragon, meaning head dragon (see the reference to Arthurian Legends in the Local Folklore section later). Celtic-British battle horns were made of metal with dragon-like heads. The Britons in Wales (Welsh being the Saxon name for foreigner) adopted the red dragon as their badge. There is folklore of the red dragon (Britons of Wales) fighting the white dragon (Saxons). The West Saxons had adopted the dragon banner by 752 A.D. Since in that year, they fought under a golden dragon banner against Mercia.

The Sutton Hoo helmet (pagan) probably dates from the late 5th century. It was placed in a royal ship burial in Suffolk in the early 7th century and contains three dragons. There is a dragon head at each end of the crest running from the front to the back of the helmet and another on the forehead of the helmet looking up between the eyes, the eyebrows forming the wings, the nose as the body and the moustache as the tail. The dragon motif was once part of royal regalia signifying power with eyes that never shut and see in all directions.

The dragon banner continued in use. King Harold of Wessex had two at the Battle of Hastings in 1066. The Bayeux Tapestry shows them, one fallen and one still flying over the huscals resisting William of Normandy's mailed cavalry and archers. At Crecy in 1346, King Edward III had a red dragon standard. The armorial bearing of the current Prince of Wales includes a dragon and the Standard of Wales is still a red dragon, although the design and style have changed over the centuries.

In recent military history, dragons (with four legs) feature in the badge of the following units: Royal East Kent (The Buffs) Regiment, Royal Berkshire Regt., Queen's Regt., West Somerset Yeomanry, Montgomeryshire Yeomanry, Monmouth Regt. The City of London Yeomanry badge had two dragons; both the Kings Royal Rifle Corps and the Royal Northumberland Fusiliers had St George killing the dragon; the Royal Army Dental Corps has the head of a dragon with a sword held in its mouth.

The gold wyvern on a black background was the sign of the 43rd Wessex Division in the Second World War. The military badge of the Wessex Division, later the Wessex Brigade, also shows the wyvern, being derived from the arms of the Kings of Wessex. The Brigade once included the Devon and Dorset Regt., Gloucestershire Regt., Royal Hampshire Regt., Berkshire and Wiltshire Regt., (these counties made up old Wessex). The Somerset Regt. being light infantry was organised differently.

There has been a recent upsurge in the interest in Wessex as an autonomous region, especially since the Queen's youngest son was made Earl of Wessex on his marriage in 1999. There is now an official flag of Wessex, which shows a gold wyvern on a red background, and is currently used to promote Wessex for tourism purposes and for various Wessex societies.

**Wessex Brigade cap badge**

In heraldry, both the gold dragon and the gold lion are royal badges. The coat of arms of Dorset has two golden wyverns representing the ancient kingdom of Wessex with the motto 'who's afear'd'. Hampshire has a golden lion, and the modern coat of arms of Somerset has a red dragon on a gold background showing that Somerset also was part of the ancient kingdom of Wessex.

Gold, red or green dragons can be found as inn or pub signs, as can golden or red lions. The colour white only seems to be used for unicorns, bucks, harts and horses on such signs, not dragons. References to green dragons appear to associate the dragon with nature in the same way as a Green Man. Both dragons and Green Men can be seen on many pre-reformation churches and were put there as a defence against the intrusion of evil.

Unicorns are mythical beasts, probably based on misunderstood reports of the rhinoceros. The unicorn's horn was supposed to have magical properties. This was possibly due to the misconceived idea, still current, of the aphrodisiac properties of rhinoceros horn. The lion and the unicorn are on the royal coat of arms, but carvings or pictures of unicorns are rare compared to those of dragons. The unicorn and the dragon were both said to be soothed by music, perhaps a folklore example of one pattern of vibrations complementing another.

Some legends refer to the sun and stars being swallowed by a cosmic dragon. Other stories refer to the World Serpent which is supposed to girdle the earth under the sea with its tail in its mouth. So long as it bites its own tail, it is calm, but if it is not, then its movement results in floods like tidal waves. Such stories, which are found worldwide, could be very ancient folk memories of earthquakes and tsunamis, former seismic events, and could refer to shifts in the earth's mantle and crust, as has been proposed by Rand Flem-Ath and Colin Wilson in *The Atlantis Blueprint*. The earth's magnetic pole is known to change position, perhaps associated with such movements in the mantle. The Economist Magazine (12th May 2007) referred to the likelihood of another change in the earth's magnetic field being due.

The movement of the earth's crust under an observer would appear to show all the stars moving towards the horizon, as if the sky were falling. Titanic forces apparently causing the sky to fall could result in dragon legends. The Romans reported that the only thing the Celts were frightened of was the sky falling.

Comets or other lights in the sky were thought to be dragons foretelling ill omen. In 793 A.D. the monks at Lindisfarne apparently saw terrible dragons of many colours flying over the island. This was seen as a bad omen and soon afterwards the Vikings raided the island, sacked the monastery, killed the monks and looted their treasure. In 1222 dragons were seen over London and terrible storms and flooding followed. Perhaps the sighting of dragons can be explained by the occurrence of lightning, especially ball lightning, also shooting stars, comets and the Aurora Borealis.

Dragons were considered to be brave and were thought to be guardians of treasure, for example at barrows (tumuli), caves and lakes. This treasure, also associated with ley focus sites, was in fact knowledge and not gold. Stories of dragons guarding barrows are more common in northern counties whereas in the south the dragon is associated more with hills, wells and stones. This is probably due to Viking Settlement in the Danelaw of north eastern England, and folklore about ley line alignments (dragon lines or earth energy lines) in southern England. The earliest dragon story in English is that of Beowulf who killed the guardian dragon at a barrow and then killed its mother dragon that lived in a lake.

Dragons were also associated with alchemy and the elements: earth, fire, air and water since they lived on earth, breathed fire, flew in the air and swam in water. Electromagnetic earthlights are reported to be seen near faults in the earth and can also have been thought of as dragons (see *Earth Lights* by Paul Devereux, 1982). It is said that all stone circles built in the Neolithic and Bronze ages are within half a mile of a fault. Such circles are found on ley lines. A geological fault is supposed to lie under Christchurch Bay and underwater sarsen stones have also been reported. Poisonous dragon breath may arise from dangerous gas and radiation from underground, now known from radon gas emerging from granite.

Herbal lore also makes use of dragon symbolism. There are several plants or part of plants such as their roots, berries, flower or leaves used in herbal medicines which have dragon nicknames ('nick' from Old Nick – the devil): flowers such as Snap Dragon, the common name for antirrhinum, Dragon Root, Dragon Herb where its leaves are used in soups and salads and the Dragon Tree whose sap is used for magical purposes, are some examples. People who take hallucinatory drugs have reported seeing enormous frightening monsters or serpents. Sometimes they can experience obtaining deeply significant insights giving new knowledge. Hallucinogens can occur naturally, as found in some mushrooms, and such experiences may account for the existence of prehistoric cave paintings and dragon myths in folklore.

Dragons often feature in street theatre. Apart from those in Chinese New Year festivals and parades, the Hobby Horse (from Hob – the devil), also known as Old Snap, appears in carnivals, as do mummers, guisers and Morris Dancers. Mummers' Plays have been performed in the British Isles for hundreds of years and are folk tales based on legends like that of St George. Mummers acted originally in silence and the performers (guisers) in disguise, possibly blackened like a chimney sweep or wearing a mask. Morris is probably a derivation of Moorish i.e. dark skinned. The Dorset Ooser was a man wearing a bull-headed, bulging-eyed devil mask perhaps acting the part of a warlock (the male witch in charge of a coven). A dragon effigy was used in street theatre at Salisbury until the early nineteenth century.

# Types of Dragon

The name dragon originates from the Greek word 'drakon' meaning serpent. Early light field guns were known as 'drakes' since they spouted flame and smoke. Mounted infantry who were armed with firelocks were known as dragoons.

The bible refers to dragons: Leviathan, the coiled sea serpent, and Rahab, the defiant one. The dragon also represented the devil. The dragon in Revelations has seven heads, ten horns and a great tail. It brought drought, sterility and famine. This is probably a contemporary reference to the city of Rome with its seven hills and of the Roman Empire using dragon banners and bringing destruction.

Mythology has many types of dragons:

**Amphisbaena**  A creature with a head at both ends of the body. Only one head slept at a time; both vomited fire.

**Apep**  The giant cosmic serpent of Egypt.

**Arachindraco**  A poisonous dragon with only two legs and a scorpion's tail.

**Asp**  A small poisonous snake or snake-like dragon with blocked ears so as not to be able to hear the pipe of a snake charmer or the words of priests.

**Aspidochelone**  A whale-like sea monster that could drag men and ships to the bottom of the sea.

**Avanc,** sometimes called **Addane**.  A serpent that lived in a bottomless lake.

**Basilisk,** also called **Cockatrice**. A cock-headed wyvern whose gaze was deadly so that it could only be viewed by use of a mirror or other reflective surface (like the polished shield of Perseus against the Gorgon). The cockatrice was supposed to be born from the egg of a seven year old cock (which of course does not lay eggs) and incubated by a toad (cold blooded) on a dung hill.

**Bigorne** A medieval mythical dragon who ate obedient husbands and grew fat because so many men obeyed their wives. Dominant women today can still be referred to as 'dragons'.

**Chimera** A grotesque monster with a lion's head behind which was a goat's head, a goat and lion's body with the hind part a dragon.

**Dragon** A fire-breathing crocodile with bat-like wings, a barbed tail and which could have horns and ears. Sometimes it has a face or a head on the tail and spikes on its body. There might also have been roundel marks on the body containing extra eyes. As a result of the roundels, peacock feathers have been mistaken for the marks of a dragon. According to Greek mythology, the peacock was the physical representation of Hera, Queen of the Gods. Superstition still exists with peacock feathers and folklore maintains they are either unlucky or a sign of good fortune, depending on the culture. Some dragons had nine coils, based on the Celtic magic number of three times three.

The dragon was also supposed to be generated from rotting flesh as found on battlefields, although the raven was usually the scavenger which cleaned up stricken fields.

**Drake** Another name for the dragon.

**Fire-Drake** was a fearsome dragon, fifty paces long and serpentine in nature, that lived in a cave and guarded a large hoard. Fire-Drake was the dragon with which Beowulf battled.

**Gryphon** or **Griffin** has the head, claws and wings of an eagle but the body, hind legs and tail of a lion. It is supposed to be able to fly higher than any other creature and has the reputation of a guardian; hence sometimes it is used as a symbol for Christ.

**Guivre** Another name for a worm, a legless and wingless dragon, which originated in England and lived in forests or wells or anywhere near water.

**Harpy** A creature with a beautiful face, head, hair and torso but the body of a serpent or dragon. It robs men of their chastity or if it has a male face with a beard, it represents avarice.

**Hobby Horse** A name given to dragons used in Mummer's Plays, also called

Old Snap from the noise of its artificial jaws, and derives from Hob, a name for the devil, which in turn has derived from Lugh, the Celtic god.

**Hydra**  The nine-headed dragon.

**Knucker**  This is the name of a worm which lived in deep (bottomless) pools known as knucker holes. These were common in the south of England and one such knucker hole was near Lyminster Church in Sussex. The dragon that lived here was slaughtered by the hero who claimed the hand of the daughter of the King of Sussex as a reward.

**Lamia**  Similar to a Harpy but it eats children.

**Leviathen**  A giant coiled sea serpent which was able to go on land (like the Christchurch dragon).

**Lindworm**  A wingless and legless dragon, i.e. a worm or serpent, which can have a scorpion's tail, and eats corpses. It can live in the earth and in lime trees but, like the eel, eventually returns to the sea.

**Mantichore**  A man-faced lion who eats humans and seduces from virtue.

**Mermaid**  The top half of this fabulous creature is a beautiful woman and the bottom half is a fish. The mermaid can represent prostitution.

**Mermaid Dossier, Christchurch Priory Church**

**Midgard Orm** also called the **Orurabores** or **Jomangand**, the world serpent which lies coiled around the globe with its tail in its mouth.

**Naga** These were semi-divine snakes with human faces, a body like a serpent and no wings. They are thought to originate from India or the area which is now Pakistan and lived in a watery region under the earth. Nagas were patrons of water and clouds and could cause flooding or drought if disturbed. In some stories Nagas can change from human to snake form and vice versa at will.

**Nicor** A sea serpent which coils up and down, unlike a snake, with left and right movement. In Scandinavian mythology, he was a sea monster that ate sailors.

**Nidhaggar** Lives in the earth and eats the dead.

**Nidhogg** The dragon serpent which lives in the roots of Yggdrasil, the World Tree, and gnaws at its roots.

**Ophion** A giant serpent coiled seven times round the cosmic egg laid by the 'Goddess of All Things'; from the egg hatched the universe.

**Pard** A spotted fierce creature with a beard and a snake's tail. (A leopard was thought to be born of a lioness and a pard.)

**Peiste** A water horse, probably based on stories of the hippopotamus, a creature to be feared.

**Phoenix** A bird which lives one at a time and for 500 years. It grows from fire in its nest.

**Rahab** The dragon referred to in Job 7.12 and Isaiah 51.9.

**Salamander** The mythical beast can be spotted, has a forked or knotted tail, is very poisonous and can pass through or live in fire. The creature is usually portrayed as green. (Salamanders are real amphibians which live in water, swampy ground or in rotting wood and have the ability to regenerate any limbs they have lost. The giant salamander is found in Japan and China and can grow up to 6 feet in length.)

**Francis I, King of France used the salamander as his insignia**

**Serpent** There are many different kinds both real and mythical. In mythology they are used both to represent the devil and also wisdom and self-renewal, the latter because of the serpent's ability to shed its skin and so grow.

In pagan times, snakes were regarded as guardians and symbols of fertility due to their phallic shape and their skin-shedding ability. House snakes could be kept, able to live in a hole near the hearth and fed on milk including, allegedly, human milk. These snakes could be regarded as representing the Earth Mother. Large glass beads or round stones were called 'serpent's eggs'. Snakes driven from their holes by floodwater gave rise to dragons being associated with floods.

The Oracle at Delphi in Greece, associated with wisdom, was held in a large cave with resident snakes and conducted by a priestess known as the Python.

Two serpents twined round the wand of Asklepois (a doctor) gave rise to the Caduceus, a sign for health, now seen also to represent the double helix of DNA.

Besides those mentioned above other types of serpents include:

Cerastes (horned)

Dipsa (its bite causes death by thirst)

Emorris (its poison makes the victim bleed to death)

Hypnale (it kills victim by deep sleep)

Jaculus (it throws itself from trees onto its prey)

Prester (its bite causes instant putrefaction and great swelling)

Scitalis (so brightly coloured that it makes all stop to look at it)

Seps (its bite dissolves flesh and bone)

Shamir (the stone-splitting serpent that helped Solomon build his temple)

Tempter (the Garden of Eden's serpent, sometimes shown with a woman's face)

Webber (a house snake fed on human milk, seen as a dragon by Christian missionaries)

Viper (practices unnatural sex)

White (its poison works so fast that the victim is dead before the bite is felt)

**Serra** A swordfish with wings and a crested spine. It is credited with being a sea dragon able to sink ships.

**Siren** A fabulous creature which is half bird and half fish. It has a beautiful feminine voice with which it lures men and then eats them.

**Sphinx** A creature with a human head, a lion's body, the wings of an eagle and the hind feet of a bull. It is often portrayed as female.

**Tatsu** The Japanese dragon which can change its size and become invisible.

**Unicorn,** also known as **Monoceros.** It has the head and body of a horse, the hind legs of a stag, the tail of a lion and has one long single horn in the centre of its forehead. Legend has it that the unicorn could be tamed by a female virgin who could place her girdle around its neck to lead it. The unicorn myth was based on stories of the rhinoceros. Sometimes a narwhal horn was taken for a unicorn's horn.

**Worm** This is one of the most common dragons to appear in British folklore (such as the Lambton Worm of Northumberland or the Linton Worm of Cornwall). The name comes from the Anglo-Saxon word 'orm'. The Great Orm Peninsular in North Wales is on a long distance alignment to Portland Bill, Dorset, passing over many ancient sites; such alignments are leys or dragon lines. The worm is wingless and scaly with no arms or legs. It is very similar to a gigantic snake, has the added characteristic of poisonous breath and can spit venom or spew poisonous gas. It could also crush its enemy in its massive coils. The worm was able to regenerate after being cut into pieces and was very difficult to kill.

**Dossier of 2 Wyverns, Christchurch Priory Church**

**Wyvern** The Wessex dragon. The name is associated with the Saxon word 'orm' (later derivations: worm, wurm, wyrm, verm, vermin and also wibber, wipia, viper) meaning serpent. The wyvern has a dragon's head, wings and front legs but no back legs, and a large strong looped tail; it is depicted as a dragon with the rear-half a serpent and wings of a bat. The Wyvern was feared in medieval times for its wickedness and the disease it was supposed to spread in northern Europe.

**Yale** This creature was as big as a horse and had the tail of an elephant and horns that could swivel back and forth.

16

# Dragon Energies

Dragons can be associated with energy known as 'earth energy'. (This energy has also been given various names at different times and places including: odyle, vril, orgone, ond, nwyvre, nwyfre, vouivre and nwyf). The energy lines, ley lines, which are supposed to pass over or through the earth are sometimes called dragon lines because dragons are supposed to fly in a straight line. These lines are the straight-line networks stretching for many miles that connect ancient sites of spiritual, ceremonial or cultural interest, such as stone circles and standing stones, burial mounds, henges and pre-reformation churches as well as natural features like sacred hills or lakes. Ley lines have proved difficult to define and still remain largely unexplained although the most likely scientific explanation is that of farming calendars. Some people attach a mystical significance to leys; others accept that there can appear to be a change in the earth's magnetic field along such lines, and that possibly humans once used them to aid navigation in ancient times as maybe birds, fish and animals still do.

Pre-reformation churches on ley lines often have carvings of dragons. Perhaps they represent energies used to defend the holy site. Examples can be found in Christchurch Priory Church (see the chapter on Christchurch Priory dragons). Such early churches are frequently located on pre-Christian pagan sites, since in 601 A.D. Pope Gregory ordered churches to be built on pagan sites where people had been used to worship.

Dragons are also associated with spirals and their tails are often shown in loops or coils. Nine coils are sometimes shown, the important triple number of three times three. Circles can indicate the passage of a year and spirals can indicate time. Loops, coils and labyrinths can be associated with movement and time. Glastonbury Tor has coils around it but these were for agricultural use although the church on top was dedicated to St Michael the dragon killer. Chinese mythology refers to lung mei, dragon paths, which channel the magnetic energies of the earth and cosmos.

**Man pulling tail of two-headed dragon**
**Christchurch Priory Church**

The likelihood is that ley lines were actually Neolithic farming calendars. Farmers needed a calendar to know when to plough, sow, harrow, irrigate and harvest and also when to move animals onto or from grazing land, either in areas otherwise liable to flood or on exposed hills. Reading and writing skills were not available in prehistoric Britain, hence straight line alignments were used as calendars, by setting markers as back sights to observe sun rise at horizon features at key dates in the farmer's year. For example: dates near Imbolc (2nd February), Spring Equinox (21st March), Beltaine (1st May), Summer Solstice (21st June), Lughnasa (2nd August), Autumn Equinox (23rd September), Samhain (1st November), Winter Solstice (22nd December). Many of these dates were later adopted by the Christian church. Christmas Day, for example, is the day on which the return movement of the sun towards the north is apparent. Fires were lit on hilltops at dawn on such key dates to welcome and strengthen the sun. Perhaps these fires were also used as calendar signals. Bones were added to these fires, especially at the festival of Samhain, as the smell of burning bones was supposed to drive off dragons and evil spirits. This is the derivation of 'bonfire'.

Ley alignment markers include megaliths (standing stones), dolmens (stone tombs) and long barrows (ossuaries for the bones of important ancestors). Long barrows could be orientated to admit a sunbeam at a key date, to symbolise the Sky Father penetrating the Earth Mother. Tangents to stone circles or henges or an outlying stone could also be markers. Often alignments do not enter the circle perhaps because it is thought to be either holy or polluted. Sometimes circles which are penetrated by shadow from a standing stone were used for ritual, such as at Stonehenge with the helestone and the central trilithon. Perhaps the concept of a virgin's girdle calming the unicorn relates to stone or henge circles. A henge could also be the focus for several alignments, as at Knowlton Church Henge at Cranborne Chase in Dorset. Bronze Age round barrows and settlement sites can also appear on such alignments. The deep ditch around a henge may be linked to ley lines which are usually tangential to the henge or stone circle or go to an outlier stone. This may be due to the ditch being intended to trap energy or some ritual creation and so prevent its escape. Ley line markers sometimes attracted long-term fertility and religious rituals, and later still some became the sites for Christian crosses, chapels or churches. Megaliths and barrows were often thought by Saxon invaders to be places where there was buried treasure and hence guarded by a dragon. The treasure existed but it was knowledge rather than bullion. The treasure, probably once secrets which gave power to a ruling elite of priests or kings, was that of the religious and fertility rites associated with the farming calendar.

The Devil's Den is all that remains of a Neolithic burial chamber and is found on the road from Marlborough to Avebury in Wiltshire. Silbury Hill is part of the complex system of Neolithic monuments around Avebury, which also includes the West Kennet Long Barrow. Silbury is the tallest pre-historic man-made mound in Europe and it is thought to be a Harvest Hill, representing the pregnant belly of the Earth Mother near which rises the River Kennet, associated with another body part. All these places lie on ley lines.

Avebury is an ancient stone circle, a near neighbour of the younger Stonehenge. Both were obviously very important as religious centres and the massive avenue of each leads straight down from the circle to the River Avon (Avon being a Celtic name for river). Avebury stone circle dates back to the Neolithic Stone Age some six thousand years ago.

The Hampshire Avon, which flows past Stonehenge to Christchurch, is named for the Earth Mother goddess of the pre-Celtic, pre-Indo European inhabitants of what became Wessex. They had several names for water and all water came from the Earth Mother. One Earth Mother title was Ver, hence the Avon name is derived from a'ver(n), belonging to the Mother.

The Giants Dance of Sun and Earth are built into structures like Stonehenge and Newgrange. This is mirrored by the circular fertility dances of folklore and recalled by place names which mention dancing, weddings and making merry, also by whirling dances at stone circles and standing stones which perhaps were intended to tap into energy in the earth. This could even have been the case with religious processions which moved sun-wise around and within churches. Fire was once lit by using a spinning axle, a whimble, to generate heat from friction. There is a Whimble Stone on a summer solstice alignment from the Waterstone (dolmen) on the Mendip Hills.

The intersection of focus points of ley lines could have become religious sites, first pagan later Christian. This appears to have occurred at locations such as Christchurch Priory Church at the confluence of the rivers Avon and Stour (the place where rivers meet was often a sacred site in many cultures) and the medieval chapel site at St Catherine's Hill, Christchurch, Dorset. Some other notable ley focus points in Dorset were at the southeast end of the Hengistbury Head promontory (now eroded by the sea), Knowlton Church Henge at Cranborne Chase and at Cerne Abbas with its Giant. Such locations often have dragon folklore. Examples of some local dragon or ley lines are given in the Appendices.

A ley line calendar representation exists in the Union Flag of Great Britain showing the red on white, north-south (sun at zenith) and east-west (equinox) cross of St George merged with the diagonal white on blue (solstices) cross of St Andrew, also the diagonal red cross on white of St Patrick. The diagram at Appendix 5 is an example. Other crosses have similar properties: the Maltese cross is created by joining midsummer sunset and sunrise, Beltaine and Imbolc sunrise, midwinter sunrise and sunset and Imbolc and Beltaine sunset. A tau cross is the equinox line perched on the noon line.

There can be a connection between dragon/energy lines and certain sites since lightning frequently strikes at the same place (e.g. hilltops, prominent stones, church towers or steeples). This is why some buildings have a lightning conductors built into them. Where a lightning bolt strikes there is a slight change in the local magnetic field. This can be detected by some sensitive people and by dowsing. Therefore energy changes can occur at stone sites which were also used as calendar markers.

Earth energies are thought to be telluric currents, which are very low frequency electric currents that occur naturally in the surface layers of the earth's crust. They are induced by changes in the earth's magnetic field and can be affected by electro-magnetic fields and influences from outside the earth such as from the sun. These influences constantly change as the position of the earth relative to the sun changes as the earth moves around the sun while spinning on its axis. The intensity of telluric currents is said to be sufficient to drive air movements that create atmospheric electricity. It is likely that human bodies and brains can react to these currents. After all the gravitational pull of the moon creates tides and supposedly affects lunatics.

Standing stones in Britain and elsewhere often appear to be aligned on astronomic events such as sunrise or sunset, moon standstills, the appearance of Venus and other planets and constellations. It may be that stones were thought to act as magnetic antennae to attract cosmic radiation and store the electro-magnetic energy that would encourage plant growth and enrich local farmland. Perhaps this was one reason for the Egyptian needle-like obelisks that were set into the ground. Some standing stones still survive e.g. at the site of the old Hordle Church in Hampshire there are two fallen sarsens, at Winterbourne Abbas in Dorset a stone circle, and on Purbeck several megaliths, but many must have been removed over the six thousand years of intensive human occupation. Perhaps there were once such stones where churches now stand. Some churches do have what were once standing stones built into them.

Alignments can create geometric shapes on the landscape and sometimes ancient sites appear at regular intervals from each other perhaps using multiples of Professor Thom's megalithic yard. An example is the right-angled triangle (5, 12, 13) discovered by Robin Heath with its base the alignment from the Isle of Lundy to Stonehenge, a distance of 123.4 miles, via Glastonbury Tor and another alignment from the tump at the halfway point on Lundy due north to Caldy Island and onto the bluestones quarry at the Prescilly Mountains in Wales, the source of the bluestones of Stonehenge.

The observation point from which to view the sun at dawn or sunset, or standstills of the moon, against a hill or col feature could be extended across the landscape by several mark points. Long alignments can exist e.g. Great Orm in north Wales to Portland Bill in Dorset. Lines over such distances have to curve slightly on a two-dimensional map representing the three-dimensional curved surface of the earth. Some of these long distance alignments are indicated by the use of 'Michael' names or Michael derivatives for churches and ley alignment markers. An example is the line from Skellig Michael off Ireland to Mount Carmel in Israel. Another is from Cornwall to Lincolnshire via Glastonbury and Avebury. Lincoln Cathedral has a pair of dragons above its west door.

**Chevrons carved in Christchurch Priory Church**

God as the Lord of Light would be able to be expressed in light alignments and in number and geometry. Farming calendars would enable God to be perceived in nature in the cycle of fertility: reproduction, death and new life. Time is expressed as an annual cycle and represented as a circle or spiral. Sometimes it is associated with the coil of a serpent, hence the use of fossil ammonites in some structures including churches. Chevrons carved in early churches, like Christchurch Priory, may be intended to represent waves, perhaps of the sea or of sound or of vibrating light from the sun.

Some ancient place names refer to light (lot) and alignments (camu) as bent or curved (light) since following the surface of the earth, with words like Camelot (South Cadbury) and Camulodumum (Colchester). The Celtic god's name Lugh is linked to light. Lugh was referred to as the 'Shining One' as in 'Lugh of the Shining Hand' or Silver Hand. He symbolises the triumph of good over evil and light over darkness, but the church saw him as a devil since he was a pagan god, his attributes of light and a spear were apparently transferred to St Michael, the dragon killer.

**Stained glass window showing St Michael slaying a Dragon**

The bent light expression may also relate to the use of crystal or glass lens to generate fire by light from the sun on midsummer's day, to rekindle fires in a sun worship ritual on the longest day of the year. Such a curved lens (monstrance) may be the basis for the legend of the Holy Grail, which has been described as a bowl or chalice because of its shape.

The idea of a beam of light may be the origin of the magic spear of Lugh, which was said to flash fire. Spears also occur in legends with St Michael, and later St George when they slew or tamed dragons (the devil).

Lugh's attributes included knowledge, magic, learning, skills, travel and trade. It is possible that Christianity associated him with the Archangel St Michael who, besides leading the Heavenly Host, was also a kind-hearted personality. Lugh as a sun god (control of sunbeams) may have been associated with the spear of Michael (control of the dragon, hence of earth energies).

Like Lugh and Michael, the Greek god Apollo also had a spear. He is reported as being worshipped in Britain at the nineteen-year lunar cycle by the playing of harps at a stone circle, perhaps Stonehenge. Legend states that he defeated Python at Delphi.

Many ancient myths relate to gods or heroes killing dragons. Other examples include:

Zeus, king of the Greek gods, who defeated Typhon and imprisoned it in a volcano.

Herakles (the Greek Hercules) killed the seven-headed Hydra.

Cadmus (also Greek) who killed a dragon and sowed its teeth which grew into armed warriors.

Jason (also Greek) also sowed a dragon's teeth.

Sigurd, a German hero, killed the dragon Fafnir

Ragnor Lodbrok, a Norweigan king killed a dragon

Sir Percival (Celtic Peredur), one of Arthur's knights, killed a serpent dragon.

Celtic Christianity developed in Britain in the years before the arrival of Roman Catholic Christianity in the seventh century. The Druids had a god Mabon, a young man who died for his people. They believed in reincarnation, hence had no fear of death. The story of Christ, his death and resurrection was thus easy to accept. The Arthurian legends include stories of Merlin, his magician and adviser who bears a strong resemblance to a Druid. So other Celtic beliefs are also likely to have influenced Christianity in Britain, and even emerged in monastic lifestyles e.g. tonsures. Celtic beliefs in monstrous beasts like dragons will also have influenced artists working in churches, where biblical stories were represented visually as aids to teaching and understanding at a time before the general use of reading and writing.

Arthur, the British war leader, was not popular with the church, probably because he used church property to finance his costly mailed cavalry; also because he may have hung a brother of the contemporary historian Gildas for piracy, so Gildas never gave Arthur credit. The story of Arthur, Guinevere and Sir Lancelot may be a pagan memory of matriarchy and of the Earth Mother being fertilised by sunlight from the Sky Father. We know that the sword in the stone tale refers to Bronze Age technology, which occurred long before Christian Arthur was born.

The oriental concept of Feng Shui is an ancient Chinese discipline dating back at least 3,000 years, based on the understanding of the dynamic flow of energy throughout the universe. Such energy lines probably relate to the aerial dragons of Chinese mythology. Today it is the art of using the environment to influence the quality of a person's life improving their health, wealth and vitality.

Feng Shui was first used to determine the best place for tombs. Later it was used to site monuments, palaces and government buildings and more recently whole cities have been designed and built according to Feng Shui principles.

# Dragon Stories

The Christian church referred to the devil as a dragon and included dragon-type mythical beast carvings in churches. Many of the dragon stories immortalised in folklore have their basis in the early struggle of Christianity over paganism and its success due to the heroics of a saint.

The idea of a terrifying beast was taken literally, due to references in the Bible to dragons (see the Book of Revelations), and also in storytelling as an entertainment in a time before books. No one could read and write in Britain until after the Roman invasion and even then only a few. Before the invention of the printing press, storytelling was an essential part of community life, whether in the family circle or in wider social groups. The absence of literacy limited the ability of people to secure an education for themselves, with critical capabilities. The education of a Celtic Druid (Brahmin-type role) took over 19 years and consisted of learning by rote. Even when literacy skills became available, they were mostly confined to a hierarchical conservative clergy until after the Reformation, and even then, excluding the churchmen, were largely confined to a limited number of males in wealthy families until after the end of the 18th century.

Before writing became common, stories would be passed on orally down the generations. As a result, the tales could become confused. A successful leader who defeated an enemy or who lead his people through a calamity like a famine, flood or earthquake could become a dragon killer over the passage of time.

The movement of troops and traders across the Roman Empire provided a vehicle for dragon stories to circulate over wide areas. The development of long distance sea travel from Western Europe to Africa, India and China also provided sailors with stories about unusual beasts, which were embroidered into tales of monsters and passed down through the generations.

Dragon myths could also account for a change in circumstances. The Celtic

Britons who lost land to the invading Saxons had folklore to explain this. Two dragons which had been captured at the centre of the island in Oxford were taken in antiquity and buried at Dinas Emrys in Snowdonia. Years later when Britons were under pressure from the Saxons, the boy Merlin was taken there to be sacrificed. Before the sacrifice took place, Merlin, using his great visionary powers, caused the Britons to excavate a hole and find the dragons which fought there. The white dragon, the Saxon, defeated the red dragon, the Celt. Hence, what happened to the Welsh was preordained so they were not to blame for the English conquest.

Pictures of dragons appear in medieval records and documents from monastic houses and estates. The Hampshire Record Office has some such documents in its possession. The Mottisfont Rental and the pipe rolls, the estate records of the bishops of Winchester, for example, have many illustrations of fabulous creatures; wyverns, worms and nagas all feature. These creatures were drawn deliberately unreal, though there are passing resemblances to the lion, the eagle and the snake. The scribes who drew these creatures seem to be familiar with mythical beasts, which they had probably seen in bestiaries - moral tales of birds and animals, elaborately illustrated and full of Christian symbolism. Perhaps they were based on the Physiologus which was written in Greek in about the fourth century and used stories from ancient Indian, Hebrew and Egyptian sources.

The fossil bones of dinosaurs gave credible evidence of dragons, especially the large bones and skulls found of unknown animals. Such bones appear in fossils on the Isle of Wight and in Dorset. The Roman villa at Brading on the Isle of Wight has a mosaic which includes a fabulous gryphon-like beast, perhaps based on the fossils found in that area. There is an ammonite in the church at Avebury, inside the great Neolithic henge, which was probably perceived as a coiled serpent dragon. There is also a carving of a conquered dragon on the font in the church and also at Ramsbury, once the site of a Saxon cathedral.

Other carvings in early churches include Green Men, which, like dragons, relate to pagan beliefs. The Green Man represents the spirit of nature; his head is usually male and has foliage emerging from his hair and some or all of the orifices of his face. The appearance of these carved foliate heads in ancient churches is an indication of the tenacity of pre-Christian symbolism. It is possible that the Green Man is a survival of the representation of the Celtic god Cernunnos, god of the wild wood. Cernunnos was usually shown with the antlers of a stag, which the animal sheds and re-grows every year, as the symbol of the cycle of fertility. A silver bowl found in Denmark shows Cernunnos with his antlers, wearing a torc round his neck and in the yogic posture adopted by Shiva, the Indian Hindu deity. Analysis of the bowl has shown that the silver was mined in what is now known as Romania and roughly mid-way between India and Western Europe. Some Celtic folk tales or religious myths appear to mirror those of Hindu lore. Possibly the Celts and Hindus once shared a belief system from a common ancestral source.

**Green Man**
**Christchurch Priory Church**

The Green Man could be Pan, who was also associated with fertility and performed cruel pranks, like the Viking god Loki. Pan is sometimes shown with goat's horns, beard and hind legs because of his sexual activities. Pan has given his name to Pokesdown (Pan's Hill), in Bournemouth. Perhaps Ramsdown at Hurn in Christchurch is also named after him.

**Mask of Pan**

The Celtic folklore of Herne the Hunter and the Wild Hunt probably originates in the myths of Cernunnos. The place name Cerne, in Dorset, is likely to be associated with this god and is well known for its giant cut into the hillside. The Cerne Giant is a large Green Man (or wodewose), his bare body carved in outline by removing grass from the chalk beneath so that the Giant's body is green. When scouring the outline during a cleaning operation, about 100 years ago, his manhood was exaggerated by incorporating his navel by mistake. This is unfortunate since the navel and nipples set out a 3:4:5 right-angled triangle. This special formation had important implications for prehistoric man and is the basis for creating stone circles which are usually either ellipse or ovoid (egg-shaped) in plan.

Many old East Anglian churches feature a carving of a wodewose - a wild man of the woods, bare and with long unkempt hair and a beard. He can often be found above the entrance to the church in the porch and usually in battle with a wyvern. Almost invariably he is wielding a club. The Cathedral at Quimper in Brittany has a scaled stone wodewose that is carrying a club in his right hand and a shield in his left.

**Wodewose carving in Christchurch Priory Church**

30

There is a carving of a wodewose on a bench end in the Great Quire at Christchurch Priory Church. Like the Cerne Giant, he is naked apart from some foliage and a single girdle belt (perhaps to hold fire-lighting equipment in the small of his back as was found with the Bronze Age iceman in the Alps) and holds a club (World Tree?) in his right hand. His left hand holds a shield with a face on it. The Cerne Giant once held a severed head by its hair in his left hand and had a cloak, like Hercules' lion skin, draped over his left arm.

The Cerne Giant may reflect Phoenician influence relating to their god Solen Baal. The name may have given us the word Solent for the sea channel between the Isle of Wight and the South Coast and the word Ballard at Ballard Down on the Isle of Purbeck. Some believe that the Giant is Nodens, a Celtic god of the hunt; the head in his left hand shows him as a head-hunter. Others suggest he is a post-Commonwealth send-up of Cromwell.

It is possible that the Green Man's role as 'spirit of Nature' was later taken up by St George, so much more acceptable to the Church, as in Mummers' Plays in which St George (symbolising nature) dies and lives again (thanks to the Doctor) and kills the Turkish Knight (signifying winter's end). The plays illustrate the struggle of good against the forces of evil and the theme is the continuing cycle of death and resurrection. In some plays, the main character is called Green George.

# Saints and Dragons

Various saints had adventures with dragons, in particular Michael, George and Margaret. St Michael, the Archangel, Leader of the Heavenly Host, was the most senior. His name is made up of three words from the area which became Mesopotamia, Mi Ka El meaning 'like unto God'. He could be the Sumerian god Marduk. As the most senior angel, it was appropriate for him to be regarded as a dragon killer, since the dragon represented evil. Christians in Britain tended to consecrate churches to Michael on high ground and at locations where paganism was particularly tenacious.

It is proposed by Paul Broadhurst (*Green Man Dragon*, 2006) that the name George links to gorge (entrance to the underworld) and to go for god and or light. It could be that 'orgy' suggests fertility sex rites and 'urge' gives natural desires. Og was a name for the sun god (also Gog) and his wife, the moon, Magog. Another name for the sun god is Ugh from which we get Lugh, the Shining One, who is linked to Michael. Lugh and Michael both carry spears, perhaps the spear of light, (the name of Lancelot). Celtic spears had metal to balance at the butt end, hence both ends of the spear had an iron tip and therefore an earthing capability.

Michael has also been linked to Apollo as they were both celebrated at high places and were dragon slayers. They are also associated with stories of moving stones and earthlights. The twin sister of Apollo, named Artemis or Athena is linked to Catherine. Chapels to St Catherine are often found near a Michael site such as St Catherine's Hill Chapel, Christchurch, and St Michael's Church, Sopley, which the hill overlooks.

Michael was supposed to weigh the souls of the dead to aid judgement. He was also able to intercede for them and argue their case. He was a protector of pilgrims and travellers (like the Celtic god Lugh).

Michael was often portrayed as pinning the dragon to the ground with a metal-headed spear or attacking it with a sword. Like George, whose legend came to replace aspects of that of St Michael later, he was usually shown as a mounted knight in armour on horseback, riding the dragon down. The spear used by Michael and George is often shown at an angle approaching 30 degrees west of north (330 degrees on the compass rose) with the head pointing roughly towards the Winter Solstice (approximately 150 degrees), the sun's birthday. St Michael is celebrated on 29th September, a date near the autumn Equinox, when the sun is becoming weaker. Perhaps Michael is intended to give support to the sun.

**Stone carving of winged St Michael
Sopley Church**

St Michael's Church at Sopley is built next to the River Avon but on a large mound which may have been artificially enlarged or sculpted. It is low-lying for a Michael church and may indicate pagan activities requiring to be overcome by a powerful saint. Three leys meet at this church.

The entrance to the church on the north side (the devil's side) has a carving of St Michael over the door holding his sword in front of him, hilt uppermost, in the form of a cross. On the exterior of the north transept, there are interesting and comparatively rare carvings called shelia-na-gigs. On the northwest corner there is a male and on the northeast corner a female. These grotesque sexual displays are, like Green Man carvings also found in churches, of a very ancient pagan origin. They represent defiance and insult, flourishing sexual organs at the enemy (the devil) rather like the tamer 'mooning' in hooligan culture today and expressing the well-known two-word phrase rendered in polite English as 'go away!'. Inside the church, along the north aisle, is a carved stone head shown sticking its tongue out. This is still a children's playground insult. It is meant to represent the tongue as a sexual organ in the same way as a shelia-na-gig, but more politely since it is inside the church.

**Carved stone head**
**Sopley Church**

**Carved stone head**
**Christchurch Priory Church**

The north side of the church was considered to be the devil's side since the sun never rises or sets or passes overhead on that side. The idea goes back to pre-Christian sky god (sun) worship. At Christchurch Priory the monks' graveyard

34

was situated southeast of the church, the laity having the north side, which is also where the main entrance to the church, the North Porch, and meeting place for the use of lay people including the burgesses, was situated.

The legend of St George was brought to Britain by returning crusaders from the 12th century onwards, although he is first heard of in Britain in the 7th century at Iona, one of the Scottish islands. There is also a Saxon carving of St George (Michael?) at Fordington Church, Dorchester, which predates King Alfred. The likelihood is that the original George was a third century soldier who was martyred for his faith and buried at Lydda in Palestine. Crusaders believed that George had come to their aid at Antioch in 1098 and at Acre in 1191 and fought with them against the Moslems. St George was an English battle cry in the Hundred Years War with France and the code word for 'advance' at Agincourt in 1415. Near Lydda, now Lod in Israel, is the port of Joppa (Jaffa) where local folklore has the story of the Greek hero Perseus rescuing the virgin Princess Andromeda from sacrifice to a sea dragon and killing the monster. The two stories were merged and George the Christian saint was credited with killing the dragon. He is a patron saint in many countries.

The memory of human sacrifice occurs in many myths and even continues into more modern times with the practice of foundation sacrifice when a new building is constructed. Christianity reduced this to the substitution of a child's leather shoe for a real person, offered to the local deity of the site and also to provide a ghost to defend the site against other spirits (dragons). The former Horse and Groom Inn at Bargates in Christchurch, built in 1654, was found to contain a walled-up mummified cat and a small child's shoe when the building was demolished in the 1970s. This practice has now evolved into the burying of a time capsule when foundation stones of a new building are laid with some ceremony. At the construction of the Civic Offices in Bridge Street, Christchurch in 1978, a time capsule was buried in the foundations and not under the foundation stone.

The popularity of St George resulted in him becoming the patron saint of England in 1222 when Edward III founded the Order of the Garter, and his red cross on a white shield became the flag of England. According to the medieval church, George's shield, which had been virginal white, had fallen to the ground when he was wounded during his battle with the dragon and had been stained by his blood. His red cross, really a sun symbol, dates from at least the Bronze Age and probably much earlier. St George's popularity tended to usurp the position of St Michael in English churches. Like Michael, George was frequently shown as a mounted armoured knight spearing the dragon with his lance. It has been pointed out that many carvings or pictures of Michael and George show their iron-tipped spears as earthing the dragon or taming it rather than killing it. Here, perhaps is a symbol of the saint controlling earth energies.

St George's flower is the rose (the plant associated with Venus) and the rent for Christchurch Castle was one red rose a year during the Wars of the Roses. St George was made the Protector of England by Pope Benedict 14th.

His feast day was abolished in 1552 and Protestants vandalised his shrines and destroyed illustrations depicting him in their crusade to overthrow all things Catholic. Although his feast day was reinstated in 1560, it was not actively encouraged by either the church or the state, though his popularity still continued in literature after the Reformation. He is no longer an official catholic saint but his flag is still flown on St George's Day (April 23rd) at Royal British Legions and public buildings and churches.

St George's Day is a time of spring growth and renewal (fertility). The former Julian calendar would place the date closer to May Day, the actual date of which would have once been determined by the moon. The arrival of summer is celebrated on May Day. May Eve was a time of sexual licence when young people went 'a maying'. These activities, including maypole dancing, were also banned by the protestant church during the puritanical Commonwealth period.

The national day of the English adopted saint is not much observed, unlike the saints' days of Wales (David), Scotland (Andrew) and Ireland (Patrick). The latter occasion has become a particularly good excuse for a party. St George should be celebrated with seed cake (fertility) and port wine (blood) and a red rose worn (symbolising fertility and blood).

Patrick was in fact a Briton called Magonus, probably from the Romano-British villa at Winscombe near Banwell in Somerset. His name is based on his rank in the church: Pater (father) ric (chief), hence Patrick was the chief of the fathers (priests) who converted the Irish to Christianity. Patrick's grandfather Potiti was buried on Lundy in the Severn Sea where his and other early Christian inscribed memorial stones have been found. Patrick is also credited with removing all the serpents from Ireland. In fact, Ireland is snake-free because no snakes ever reached Ireland after the retreat of the last Ice Age.

**Painting of St George on roof beam**
**Christchurch Priory Church**

The other saint credited with dragon killing is St Margaret. She was supposed to have been swallowed by a dragon but used her crucifix to cut her way out of its belly thus killing the beast. Margaret churches are rare. There is one at East Wellow near Romsey in Hampshire, which King Alfred gave to his sister. It has been suggested that Margaret represents the Earth Mother and Michael the Sky Father of pre-Christian beliefs.

Besides Michael, George and Margaret other Christian saints with dragon associations are: Beatus, Carantoc, Donatus, Dubricius, Hilarion, Hilda, Keyne, Leonard, Martha, Nicholas, Petroc, Samson and Sylvester. Each is shown to overpower or kill the dragon symbolising the triumph of good over evil and of Christianity over paganism.

As well as churches, saints could also give their names to topographical features; an example is St Catherine's Hill, a common place name in Wessex. St Catherine uses the sign of the cross in her wheel, also a sun symbol.

Popular saints were also chosen as inn names. By the 18th century the George and Dragon was the most popular name for an inn or tavern. Ye Olde George Inn at Christchurch was originally the St George and Dragon Inn; the 18th century inn sign shows this. The brewers in latter years mistook the locals who referred to their pub as 'The George' for 'King George' hence the current pub's name and sign.

Some old pubs or inns bare solely dragon names, such as the Green Dragon. However, dragons, like serpents, were supposed to be fond of drinking milk rather than ale.

# Local Folklore and Dragons

Dragon lore is often about places situated on ley lines. The stories can involve alignments of some kind, as dragons were only able to fly in straight lines, associating time and light, travel and movement. Other folklore themes concern sex and fertility, healing and renewal, the devil and death. Folklore sometimes mention stones moving (such as the building stones for Christchurch Priory being mysteriously moved from St Catherine's Hill to its current site, or the Whimblestone taking milk and flowers to the Waterstone on Mendip), or stones walking to water and going for a dip or a drink which illustrates both the travel and healing theme. One such legend states that the old stone cross, situated in a field near Langton Herring in Dorset, is supposed to go for a walk to the Fleet, the lagoon behind the Chesil Beach, to dip its head in the water at midnight on New Years Eve. Further examples and explanation can be found in the following table:

**Alignments**:

Stone lines and stone circles, particularly to outlying stones of circles;

Straight lines, arrow flight, shaft and bolt (sunbeams);

Flying horse, horse or deer leaps, especially a white animal (white a sun symbol) like Pegasus the flying horse, white buck, white hart;

Earth lights, electromagnetic events, comets, ball lightning;

Changes in dimension such as the speeding up or slowing down of time with constant rapid ageing when returning to this dimension;

Spirit flight or journeys, shape changing;

Treasure (meaning secret knowledge).

**Travel**:

Fairy paths and rings, circles (endless), spirals (circles which move in a direction);

Flying, racing, leaping, jumping (memories of funeral games);

Respect for the sites of ley markers, stones moving or being thrown or dropped;

Buildings moving to other sites;

Stones associated with water, going for a swim or drinking;

Stones taking a tribute to another site.

**Fertility**:

Phallus-like standing stones, gates or portals, stones with clefts or holes (like the Whimblestone);

Walls opening or closing;

Circles, mounds, tunnels, caves, wells, springs;

Maypoles, dancing, music, orgiastic rites;

Royalty, ladies, princesses, virgins, heroes, princes, knights;

Dragons (also guardians at ley sites, associated with the devil).

**Healing**:

Bathing, washing, drinking potions (probable use of hallucinogens);

Life restored, healing, good fortune;

Rescue by saints (e.g. Michael, George, Margaret);

Quests (e.g. the Holy Grail);

Fire renewed by use of a lens (crystal) like a monstrance found in some churches;

Blessing rituals: vigil, sensory deprivation, fasting, dancing, whirling, physical exercise, chanting, use of special words or phrases.

**Devil:**

Ghosts, haunting, poltergeist, apparitions (a blocked ley is said to cause haunting);

Devil's names (e.g. The Devil's Den in Wiltshire, Old Harry Rocks off the Isle of Purbeck), giants, witches, warlocks;

Dragon names given to topographic features;

Wild hunt, black animals particularly dogs, bears, bulls, horses, ravens, crows, eagle, blue boar;

Underworld, hollow hills;

Funeral routes e.g. corpse lanes which were dead straight;

Things not understood: UFOs, crop circles, spontaneous human combustion (Christchurch had a case of this on a ley at Parley in 1613).

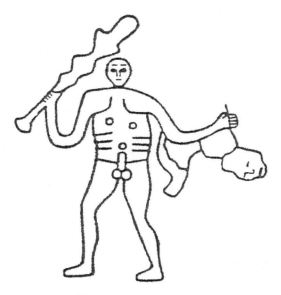

**Helis, the Cerne Giant**
**The original badge of Dorset**

There are many British legends and myths found throughout the land, perhaps the most well known are those concerning the Arthurian legends. 'King' Arthur was a British war leader who for a time staved off invasions during the period of British history after the Roman forces had left. These legends also illustrate his battle for Christianity against the pagan Saxons in Wessex. However, Thomas Mallory wrote his *Le Morte D'Arthur* in 1485 based on the old folktales and now the stories of Arthur are often depicted in the media as belonging to this period – the age of the chivalrous knight: the knights of the round table (at Winchester), Sir Lancelot, the lady of the lake and the sword in the stone contest. Legend links him with the dragon: his father was called Uther Pendragon. Merlin, the magician, prophet, and Arthur's adviser, who also features in legends, tells of the long fight between two dragons a red one (symbolising the Britons) and a white one (symbolising the Saxons).

41

Many places vie for the setting of Arthurian legends including Cornwall, Wales and Glastonbury in Somerset. One of Merlin's supposed burial places is said to be beneath Merlin's Mound at Marlborough in Wiltshire.

St Carantoc tamed a dragon that threatened Arthur at Carhampton, Somerset, and turned it into a vegetarian that only used its flames for lighting village bonfires. As a reward St Carantoc was granted by Arthur the right to build a monastery in the village. *The Anglo-Saxon Chronicle* shows that the village was subject to Viking raids during its early history.

**Figurehead from a Viking longship**

The ravaging Vikings of the late 8th to late 11th centuries may well account for more dragon legends. The figureheads on Viking longships (dragonships) were detachable wooden dragons. Sight of these and the dragonship crews were a cause of terror, as this meant that Viking raids and the destruction of their settlements by burning them down were imminent (see the story of Carhampton, above). The pagan Vikings also raided Christian monasteries and churches which were, to them, sources of easy wealth.

Wessex was first attacked by sea; the initial assault was at Portland, in Dorset, and came from Dublin by Norwegian Vikings returning to Norway by rounding Britain and travelling up the English Channel. Later attacks came from Ireland across the Irish and Celtic Seas to Somerset ravaging settlements lying along the Severn estuary; the Somerset Levels were also an easy route to penetrate inland. Vikings also came from Denmark down the Channel and up the rivers of the South Coast. The Solent and harbours like Portsmouth, Christchurch and Poole gave easy access and during this time, the Vikings destroyed Portsmouth, Southampton, Lymington and Wareham, as well as Wilton and Winchester further inland. They also occupied the Isle of Wight and twice over-wintered there. The Saxons, under King Alfred, built defences around the settlements such as at Southampton, Wilton, Shaftesbury, Christchurch and Wareham and much folklore would have arisen from these troubled times. Other Viking attacks came by land from what became the Danelaw of Northumbria, the Midlands and East Anglia.

Dragon stories from southern Wessex are heavily concentrated in Somerset, a county which was formed by Saxons, based at Somerton, from what was in the pre-Roman Iron Age part of the Durotrigian tribal area, the southern remnant of which is Dorset. Christchurch was added to Dorset as recently as 1974. The number of dragon legends in Somerset probably account for that county's badge being a dragon. Stories include:

At Kingston St Mary, a dragon was slain by a brave soul who rolled a boulder into its mouth.

At Wells, Bishop Jocelyn drove away a fierce worm-type dragon that had been terrorising the local people who lived in the area around seven holy springs. Wells Cathedral was built near this site where there had been a stone circle.

The Norton Fitzwarren Dragon was known for devouring children and destroying crops. In the 13th century, the knight, Fulke Fitzwarren, slew the dragon after a long and bloody battle. He also saved the Duke of Iberia's daughter from a dragon near Carthage while on his travels abroad. During the Iron Age, there was a battle at Norton Fitzwarren in which the battlefield was littered with bodies. The dragon was believed to have been created and risen magically from these dead bodies.

The dragon which lived in the Althelney Fens near Low Ham was a flying serpent which ate the local livestock and demanded milk. It was killed by John of Aller with a nine-foot long spear. The spear was apparently preserved in Low Ham Church and there is also an effigy to John of Aller there.

A dragon roamed between Dolebury hill fort on the northern edge of the Mendip Hills and at Cadbury-Congresbury Camp, another Iron Age hill fort in Somerset guarding legendary treasure hoards buried at both locations. There is a carving of this serpent dragon on a Saxon column now built into the wall inside Rowberrow Church. Another Dolebury Hill, near Killerton north of Exeter, also has a dragon legend.

Taunton Museum apparently has the skull of a dragon called Blue Ben who lived at Kilve and was often ridden by the devil. Ben fell off a causeway into the sea and drowned. The skull in the museum is that of an ichthyosaur.

Other Somerset places associated with dragon stories are: Brent Knoll, Castle Neroche, Church Stanton, Crowcombe, Dinder, Ker Moor, Shervage Woods on Quantocks, Trull and Wiveliscombe. Ley line alignments also pass through these locations.

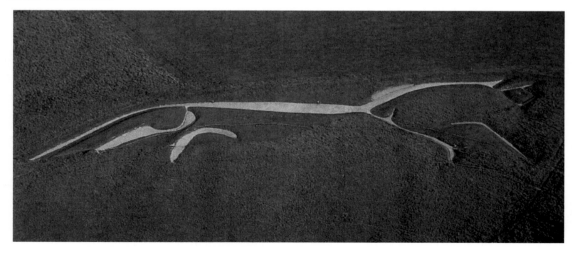

**The White Horse, Uffington**

Dragon Hill on the Berkshire Downs, close to White Horse Hill and the White Horse of Uffington is one of the sites where St George is said to have slain his dragon. The top of the hill is flat and legend has it that the blood from the dragon burnt the soil here and that is why no grass ever grows.

The Uffington white horse can best be seen from Dragon Hill close by or from above as it was carved into the shallow slope of the downs close to the top and not on the steepest slope. It is the oldest of the white horses in the area, dating back to the Bronze Age, and is of a different design to the others; much more stylised. Whether it is a horse or some other creature like a dragon is debatable, but it has been termed a horse since medieval times. It could have been cut as a tribal badge by worshippers of the sun god Belinos (Belinus) who was associated with horses. This would account why the creature was carved into the hillside where it could easily be seen from the sky. (The hobby horse of the Mummers Plays was actually a dragon.)

The dragon at Deerhurst in Gloucestershire, which had been poisoning the locals and killing their cattle, was slain by a labourer while it was sleeping in the sun after it had gorged itself on a large quantity of milk. The local church has a carving of the dragon.

At a hill fort near Stinchcombe, in Gloucestershire, is Drakestones Side where a dragon was supposed to live. Another Gloucestershire hilltop, Drakehorde, is supposed to be the site of a dragon's treasure trove.

At Southampton, Sir Bevois (Bevis) killed a dragon. Sir Bevois was a character from the 12th century who had a magic sword and a fabulous horse called Hirondelle. Sir Bevois was sold into slavery by his stepmother but later returned to England to reclaim his father's land, according to local legend, and founded Southampton. He had already performed heroic deeds including slaying two lions to protect his true love Princess Josian. These are shown protecting the Bargate on the city of Southampton's coat of arms. He was apparently responsible for building the Arundel Tower of Southampton Castle and when he was near to death, he made a wish to be buried where his sword landed after it had been thrown from the top of Arundel Tower. The spot where it landed is near Portswood at the entrance to the Bevois Valley. In another legend, Sir Bevois is a giant who can walk from Southampton to the Isle of Wight without getting his head wet.

Hampshire has its own example of a cockatrice – the Wherwell Cockatrice which allegedly hatched in Wherwell Priory. It grew into a man-eating monster and devoured several knights who tried to slay it. The dragon was eventually killed when it saw its own reflection in a mirror brandished by a local labourer.

Another Hampshire dragon at lived at Burley Beacon Hill (or Burley Castle Hill, an Iron Age fort which may have been reoccupied as a base from which to fight dragon shipmen at Bisterne) and was probably also the Bisterne Dragon. Bisterne is on the River Avon north of Christchurch in the New Forest. There is a Dragon Lane at Bisterne and there is a focus of seven ley lines north of Bisterne Farm. The Bisterne Dragon was said to have been killed by Sir Maurice Berkley, who is supposed to have covered his armour in birdlime and then powdered glass in order to resist the fire or poison of the dragon. He killed the beast but then died soon afterwards. Interestingly, the birdlime and powdered glass tale could be based on memories of the use of non-metal armour. In the 17th century English Civil War leather 'jacks', long coats of boiled leather, were important as they were flexible and light defensive garments. To this day, we refer to jackets and jackboots, knee-length cavalry boots, worn with ceremonial cavalry uniforms.

The use of such war gear is recorded in Viking times, when knee-length hauberks and mail shirts were the most valued forms of body armour. However, Ragnar Hairy Breeks, a Viking king and dragon killer, got his name from the leather and wool coat he wore, which was covered in pitch as a defensible, flexible garment lighter than metal. Ready to use armour could be produced by soaking clothes in pitch and then rolling them in sand. This is probably the origin of the birdlime and powdered glass story at Bisterne, a tale based on a real event involving Vikings in the 9th century attached to a hero of the Hundred Years War over five hundred years later.

Stories of unusual armour for dealing with dragons occur at different places. Armour with sharp blades attached is a similar concept to leather and pitch covered in sharp sand or glass and was used to kill a cockatrice near Saffron

Walden in Essex, the Sockburn Worm in County Durham and the Nunnington Dragon in Yorkshire. These were all areas, which, for a time, fell under Viking control.

Dorset has dragon legends at Kingston near Ivyton and also at Frampton. The dragon at Frampton is particularly interesting since it appears on a mosaic at a Roman villa apparently owned by Christians, as one mosaic has the chi-rho monogram. The mosaics were uncovered in the late eighteenth century, drawn and reburied. A mosaic has a damaged central roundel of a mounted man on a winged horse spearing a chimera dragon, one with a lion's head behind which is a goat's head and with a tail ending in a serpent's head. This could be the earliest representation of St Michael, the dragon killer, in Britain.

Christchurch has its own dragon legend. The cathedral at Laon in north-eastern France was destroyed by fire in medieval times. The monks there were sent around western Europe in 1113 to seek alms to help pay for the rebuilding of the cathedral. A party from Laon arrived at Christchurch but were thrown out of the town since the local church did not want to hand over any money as the building work started by Ranulph Flambard in 1094 was still underway. The men from Laon cursed Christchurch and as a result a five-headed sea dragon came and burnt down the town. A similar story is told of men from Laon being ejected from Bodmin in Cornwall and a curse resulting. The five-headed sea dragon was probably a memory of five Viking longships attacking Christchurch which, as a result of story telling over the years was erroneously attached to the four centuries later Laon curse story. Christchurch had many thatched buildings and fires were common.

The church, which became the Priory Church of Christchurch in 1149 and had an Order of Augustinian Canons ('monks') established there at the request of Baldwin de Redvers, the Lord of the Manor, had been started by Dean Flambard, who later became Bishop of Durham, as an extension of the previously existing Saxon Minster. The King of Wessex became a Christian in 625 so the Minster will have dated from a century or so afterwards, although there had been Christians in Dorset in Roman times as shown by the finds from excavations at the villas at Frampton and at Hinton St Mary. At Christchurch, the pagan Saxon cemetery was found at Bargates in 1977 as a result of a trial excavation organised by the author. These were the people Arthur and his men resisted. The boundary between Christian Briton and pagan Saxon was probably the Moors River, a tributary of the Stour, at Hurn. The name Moors probably derives from Celtic 'moros' meaning death (to cross for either side).

The thatched roofs of the old cob walled houses were a constant fire risk and all local settlements experienced several major fires, until the mid 19th century when the railway permitted the bulk transport of clay and slate tiles for building work. The manor court, the Court Leet, appointed officers whose duties included fire precautions. Christchurch had two Constables for the burgh, ten Tithing men for the hundred, a Hayward to control stray animals and the pound, who also acted as Town Cryer, a Bailiff to collect taxes and rents, an Aletaster and a Breadweigher for quality and control (weights and measures) and an Inspector of Chimneys with fire buckets and fire rakes, the latter to pull down burning thatch. The frequency of fires may well have added to the folklore about fire-breathing dragons.

Other factors which may have reinforced the local dragon tales could be a then unexplained, unusual meteorological event such as aurora borealis or a water spout, lights in the sky: a meteorite or comet, which would be perceived as an ill omen; ball lightning, which can meander along the ground or drop out of the sky, pass through windows and emerge from fireplaces, and be of various colours and sizes; earth lights have been seen over the sea in Christchurch Bay, where there is believed to be a geological fault; or Will O'Wisp lights on marshes, called fire-drake (dragon) and due to the presence of marsh gas.

The appearance of unusual sea creatures may have given rise to dragon legends: perhaps a whale washed ashore or seals appearing in the harbour or in the rivers. In recent years, a seal was seen for several days in the River Stour at Tuckton and a crocodile lived in the river for several months in the 1970s after it had escaped from a circus. Perhaps large snakes or eels were the perpetrators of local dragon legends. Eels abound in Christchurch Harbour and adders used to be common on open ground surrounding the town, such as on St Catherine's Hill, Hengistbury Head and Chewton Bunny in Highcliffe including the vicinity of the beach.

# Christchurch Priory Dragons

Dragons were sometimes associated with wells but, although Christchurch has a number of dragons and wells, those at Christchurch were not: Monks, Pure and Tutton's Wells are remembered instead for their curative properties for eyes. These wells were outside the town and hence were not polluted.

Christchurch has been inhabited for thousands of years, therefore there were thus many latrines. Also the churchyard was on the highest land in the town with graves cut into porous gravel, hence well water was not safe to drink. So people drank small beer (weak beer) or added some smuggled brandy to the water as the alcohol gave some protection from disease, although the existence of bacteria was unknown at the time.

The Priory Church at Christchurch has many dragons and strange, fabulous creatures carved in wood and stone, particularly in the Great Quire in the Misericords, in the Rood Screen and in the Nave.

At the foot of the two main pillars nearest the altar in the Nave are four stone sculptures of dragon creatures that appear to be guardians of the altar in this lay part of the church, west of the Great Quire, which was for the exclusive use of the Augustinian monks. One of the creatures is a gryphon, another a wyvern. These carvings at the two eastern end nave pillars are described thus:

**Most eastern pillar at the south side of the Nave**

At the southeast side, there is a dragon with a lion or hunting dog's head with its tongue out. It has a lion's body but with a spinal ridge. Its tail is like that of a lion but with three ends. Its head and body face the southeast towards Hengistbury Head and the Isle of Wight.

At the southwest side, the dragon has a longer muzzle, a hunting dog-type head with big ears and a very long looped tail. It has a lion-type body with a spinal ridge and feathered wings. Its tail is like a lion's but goes to its mouth from which it emerges. The body is aligned to the southwest towards the Isle of

Purbeck but its head is turned to the southeast and the Isle of Wight, which was the side of greatest danger of attack in the English Chanel from the Vikings. (It is also pointing to the concentration of leys at Hengistbury's southeastern promontory.) The Normans who extended and embellished the church were themselves north men (sons of Vikings); the memories of terrible raids must have lasted for generations.

**The most eastern pillar at the north side of the Nave**

At the northeast side, the creature has a beak and a feather-crested head, feathered wings, long ears and only two legs, each with three claws. It is a gryphon and its very long tail divides into a long double tail and each part finishes with triple ends. The head and body face to the northeast – towards the New Forest.

At the northwest side of the pillar is a wyvern. It has a dragon's head and ears and its tongue protrudes. This creature has bat wings, a spinal crest, one pair of legs each with four claws and a dragon tail which finishes in a loop with triple ends. The wyvern's head and body face northwest towards Cranborne Chase. It would be interesting to know if these dragons were once painted like much of the interior of the Priory.

Since the present church was built onto and over a Saxon Minster it may be that some of the dragons and other carvings were originally Saxon work at a time when Vikings were an active threat.

The Great Quire has many wood carvings of a variety of monsters including dragons, gryphons, wyvern, Green Men and a wodewose. The wodewose, a wild man of the woods, is carved on a bench end. There is foliage on him, otherwise he is naked except for a girdle round his middle. The carvings on the Misericords date from the 13th century.

The Priory Church has an unusually carved column above the south side of the Nave, midway at first floor level. This carving may perhaps have been associated with dragon energy beliefs about spiral energy as with the caduceus, the latter a sign for healing, originally based on serpents and the World Tree.

**Dragon with a hunting dog's head with its tongue out
(Southeast side)**

**Winged Dragon with hunting dog-type head with big ears
and long looped tail which it grips in its mouth
(Southwest side)**

**Gryphon with a beak, feather-crested head and only two legs
(Northeast side)**

**Wyvern with a dragon's head and ears
(Northwest side)**

**Grotesque animals and human head on the Rood Screen
Christchurch Priory Church**

There are stone carvings of grotesque animals on the Rood Screen which separates the Nave from the Great Quire. Altogether there are 36 animal heads and some bodies and they appear to represent lions, dogs, birds, gryphons(?), some seem to represent scaled creatures, others fierce woolly sheep. The frequent use of lion sculptures may be a link to the sun and pagan symbolism, since the lion is a sun sign. The northern end of the Rood Screen terminates with a human head with a particularly large nose. The stone screen may have replaced an earlier wood one which, no doubt, would have had carvings. A very fine Green Man is at the top of a palister at the west side of the south transept, but is obscured by the modern organ loft.

There are paintings of dragons on the roof beams of the Nave but these are obscured from view by a ceiling constructed in 1820. There are gryphons carved on some of the arches from the Nave to the South Aisles.

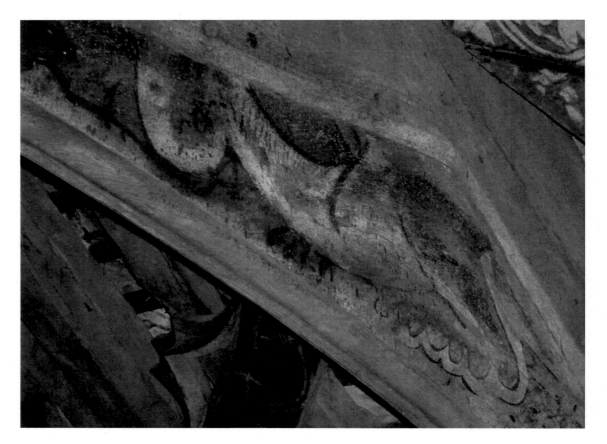

**Painting of a Dragon on a Roof Beam**

The Priory Church has a few human heads as stone sculptures inside the building. In the Nave, there is a bishop with his mitre and also a head, with a large moustache, which may once have had a hat or even a metal helmet. It has been surmised that the bishop is Ranulph Flambard, a former dean of the church. Perhaps the wearer of the grand moustache was Baldwin de Redvers, a revered Lord of the Manor in the 12th century. There is another bishop and a monk with hands crossed in the act of devotion at the northwest end of the North Porch. This porch was once the meeting place for the burgesses of the Council and the storage place for instruments of civic punishment, like the ducking stool and the whirly gig, and later the town's fire engine.

**Dossier of 2 Gryphons and a Mermaid**

**Misericord of a Demon**

**Misericord of 2 Dragons, biting each other's wings**

**A Harpy in the Great Quire**

The outside of the south side of Christchurch Priory Church has many ancient carved heads which all appear to be different. This is reminiscent of pagan Celtic head-hunting practices when severed heads were mounted on buildings. The heads of criminals were similarly mounted on town gates as a deterrent to people throughout the ages and this practice continued until the 18th century. The Priory heads are individual portraits, probably of important people. Likewise it has been suggested that the female head on the south side of the bridge at Place Mill pool is that of Isabela de Fortibus, the last of the de Redvers line who died in 1293. There is another head on the north side.

Old churches, like the Priory Church, at one time contained a monstrance, a metal sunburst on a stand, the centre of the sunburst being a glass lens. Such a lens could be used to generate fire from the sun such as on the summer solstice. Some Roman Catholic churches on the continent still have a monstrance. Their existence shows the early church recognised pagan rituals and sun alignments. Some churches were aligned to dawn on the date of the festival of the saints to which they were dedicated. Some such saints were Celtic gods given Christian attributes.

The alignment of religious structures to the sun at dawn (or set) on key festivals is known from the late Neolithic and into the Bronze Age e.g. Stonehenge and Newgrange. The mid winter solstice appears to have been the most important festival and adopted as the birthday of ancient gods, like the Roman Mithras. The idea has continued down the ages to give rise to Christmas.

# Dragons and Ghosts

Church dragon carvings and other grotesque mythical creatures, Green Men foliate heads (the Nature Spirit) shelia-na-gigs and folklore associated with dragons are all likely to occur at pre-Reformation sites, formerly pagan, on ley lines. Ghosts at some Christchurch ley focus points are as follows:

**St Catherines Hill**

An old woman in a long dress has been seen on the hill but disappears when looked for. Seven ley lines cross the site of the medieval St Catherine's Chapel on the hill inside the Roman signal station fort, the two towers of which were outside the fort but connected to each other and to the fort by a raised walkway.

St Catherine's Hill is a name likely to be derived from Kat Anne's, locally known as Katterns. Kattern Day is 25th November, halfway between Samhaim and the Winter Solstice. The saint is typically the dedication at the coastal hilltop chapels associated with pre-Christian religion, including the Earth Mother in her third form as Kali, the old woman who brings death essential for the return of new life and the cycle of fertility. She was Christianised as Katherine but in pagan times Kat Anne was the black crone, the dark side of the moon. She was celebrated on Carling Sunday, the fifth in Lent, also known as Whirling Sunday because of the whirling dances which, as with whirling dervishes, can induce trance. St Catherine's association with the wheel, a pagan fire symbol, is well known. Black peas and Kattern cakes were eaten in remembrance of the goddess.

St Catherine was also prayed to by a young woman seeking a husband.

> Sweet St Catherine send me a husband. A good one I pray.
> But a one is better than none.
> Oh St Catherine, send me your aid
> And grant that I do not die an old maid.

## Hengistbury Head

Hengistbury Head had an Iron Age promontory fort, and Barn Bight, on the shore of Christchurch Harbour, was a major Bronze and Iron Age port, possibly Britain's earliest entrêport. Here the ghost is said to be a man on horseback. The name Hengist means 'stallion'. It may be associated with the white horses of sea foam and travel linked with the Celtic god Lugh who was the god of travellers and trade. The ghostly rider may have been a 'hobbler', a light horseman, who hobbled his horse while he watched at the beacon site on Warren Hill at Hengistbury Head. Alternatively, the ghost could be a customs riding officer patrolling the coast against smugglers. This was a very dangerous occupation, since smuggling was the main local industry for many years and riding officers could be murdered, as happened at Chewton in Highcliffe. At its height during the 18th century, the largest and most audacious smuggling run to take place along the South Coast was landed at Mudeford, at the mouth of Christchurch Harbour, in 1784. There was a battle between the local smugglers with two luggers and 300 men against a Royal Navy sloop and a Customs cutter and an Excise cutter. The smugglers won by keeping the Crown vessels out of the harbour while they removed the valuable cargo and the luggers gear, although they lost the hulls.

Thirteen leys go to the southeast end of the promontory now marked by the Long Groyne, since the land has suffered greatly from erosion due to 19th century ironstone quarrying.

## Christchurch Priory Church

A major site for ghosts at a ley focus is Christchurch Priory Church, dedicated to the Holy Trinity since the Saxon Minster on the site. The Christian religion recognised the triple deity (Father, Son and Spirit), just as the pagans thought of the Earth Mother as having three forms (maid, matron and crone). The Priory is on a pagan site and a kist (stones set in the ground to make a container) of long-legged bird bones was found when the Priory House was built next to the south side of the church in the mid 18th century. The Priory is on the highest point at the confluence of the Avon and Stour rivers and was there before Christchurch Castle was built on lower land. The Saxons had a

Minster Church on the site and the location has probably been used for religious ritual since the Bronze Age. Water gods were worshipped at river junctions, and sky gods were reduced in influence towards the end of the Neolithic era by climatic changes, which arose as a result of distant major volcanic activity that obscured the sun and produced more clouds and rain. The folklore about the stones to build the church being miraculously moved from St Catherine's Hill to the current site probably dates from these times, and the technological, social and religious changes stem from the transition from Neolithic to the Bronze ages.

**Aerial View from Christchurch Priory Church
towards St Catherine's Hill**

The Priory Church ghosts are mainly 'monks' (canons) and they have been seen in St Michael's Loft (the former schoolroom above the Lady Chapel), the Great Quire, where the Augustinian canons held their services, in the Nave and at the entrance to John Draper's Chapel which is at the eastern end of the South Choir Aisle and below St Michael's Loft. John Draper was the prior at the time of the Reformation when Henry VIII ordered all monastic buildings to be destroyed. However, John Draper used his influence, as a royal chaplain, to persuade the king to return the complete church to the townsfolk of Christchurch as their parish church. In his retirement, John Draper continued to live at Somerford Grange. He was buried in front of the main altar and not at the chapel which now bears his name.

One person has also sworn an affidavit about being pushed past on the ancient spiral staircase by a presence moving to St Michael's Loft and then appearing as a visible figure in the Loft.

Figures have been seen at the former monastic precinct, in the grounds by the Porter's Lodge and on the route to Somerford Grange, by different people at various times. Processions of monks have been reported being seen both inside and outside the church. A monk has been seen seated in the Great Quire, another was seen in the Nave during services. He was seen on three occasions by a lady and each time this was followed by news of a family death.

Ghostly aromas of frankincense have been smelt in the area of the church north and south of the main altar and in the south aisle of the Nave on various occasions by different people. However, frankincense has not been used in the church since Mary Tudor was queen, although some services have reintroduced incense.

Automatic writing, in medieval French, was experienced in St Michael's Loft by a former Priory archivist and his subsequent vivid dreams concerned Stephen de Staplebrig who was a Templar sergeant monk (a mounted fighting man) who was sentenced, when the Templars were disbanded, to be a perpetual Augustinian novice at the Priory.

There are reported sightings of many other ghosts in central Christchurch and these appear to occur on ley lines, thirteen of which cross at Christchurch Priory Church.

# Leys, Place Names and Stones

There are other ley focus sites in the area where ley lines cross, or start, or end. For example, the site of the Holdenhurst Long Barrow has five leys passing through it and Wick Barrow has three. There is a suspected but unproved long barrow site with 13 leys at North Bockhampton, which was mentioned in the Christchurch Times on a report of an Archaeological Association meeting on 10th January 1861. Staple Cross has six leys. This medieval cross was situated on a mound until the by-pass altered the ground level. Tutton's Well at Stanpit has four leys, a barrow at Friar's Cliff, Mudeford, has three and the former Lob's Hole site on the coast at Chewton Bunny, Highcliffe, and now lost to erosion, had seven. Lob's Hole, a fresh water spring in Christchurch Harbour has four leys; Lugden Barrow at Dur Hill Down, once marked by a standing stone, has five; Sopley Church has three; a sarsen stone at Wootton in the New Forest has five; two sarsen stones on the site of the former Hordle Church have thirteen and a sarsen stone at Westover, Milford–on-Sea has five. Many of these sites are on the same ley lines. A large 1½ ton sarsen stone was discovered at Holdenhurst when the Spur Road was being built. No doubt it once stood on one of these ley lines. There are more to be found. Some leys converge and could create triangles, some run parallel. The focus points where leys intersect are particularly worthy of investigation. (See Appendix 4)

Some leys were marked by stones. For example two sarsen stones are at the former Hordle Church site (1080-1830) and since sarsen is not a local stone may have been brought to the location on the shore from as far away as the Marlborough Downs in Wiltshire in the Neolithic Age. Stonehenge made use of sarsen stones. Another worked sarsen stone is on a ley from the Isle of Purbeck via Christchurch Priory to a barrow in the New Forest. This is at Wootton on the Tiptoe Road east of the Rising Sun Inn at the old parish boundary between Milton and Brockenhurst.

Mark stones could often be at boundaries, as could burial sites where the ancestor's ghosts could defend the land. Prominent burial cairns gave proof of land holding and family entitlement to the farm. Unfortunately for historians many such mark stones and barrows have been lost to agriculture and to building development, in particular locally to the conurbation which has grown up to engulf Poole, Bournemouth and Christchurch. However, the existence of some can be traced as many were recorded on the 2½" and 6" Ordnance Survey maps of the late 19th century.

**The Stone Circle, Winterbourne Abbas**

The two Lob's Holes (springs) and Lugden Barrow names, mentioned above, are all remnants of the name Lugh, a Celtic god known to the Romans as Mercury, the Greeks as Hermes and to the Egyptians as Thoth. The name Lugh can be recorded in different areas as Lob, Lod, Lot, Lud, Lug, Ugh, Ug, Og, Hob, Hod, Llew and Lir. There is a Hod Hill in Dorset, which is the site of an Iron Age hill fort later used by Romans; there is Ludgershall in Wiltshire with its castle, church and medieval cross. Hobourne is an area east of Christchurch where there was once Hobourne Hill Common, and its name has been derived, no doubt, from Hob's Bourne, the original name of the Bure Stream which flows through Hobourne and into Christchurch Harbour at Mudeford. The area once called Bure, from Bower, beautiful garden, was renamed Friars Cliff by 20th century estate agents.

Derivations of the god's name Lugh, also known as the Shining One, occur as Ugh or Og, a name for the sun god. A meadow west of the Avon at Christchurch is called Ogber, perhaps named for the sun and the burgh (the fort of Saxon Christchurch). Since the names of pre-historic gods can survive in local place names it is not surprising that folk stories of dragons have also survived into the present day.

It has been suggested that stones were used to control, attract, focus or reinforce energies and to act as if earth acupuncture sites. Some people believe in dark energies which need to be earthed and managed as with Feng Shui beliefs. This could account for the images of St Michael or St George using his spear's iron head (or butt) to tame (earth) rather than kill the dragon.

If the dragon and the Green Man both represent natural energies, which need to be understood, and the Green Man is also St George who is also St Michael and Michael is Lugh, who is also Mercury, Hermes and Thoth, then all these gods, powers, saints and energies are one; just different names from different perspectives in knowledge, culture, time and space. All represent the natural energies and potential of nature, created by one loving Creator God. So all dragons are within us, for each of us to tame using the knowledge they offer.

# Note to Appendices

Leys are indicated by straight lines linking Neolithic and Early Bronze Age sites. They can also be tangential to Iron Age Hill Forts. This may indicate pre-Iron Age activity at such prominent hills, for example as astronomical alignment horizon markers. In myth, only dragons fly in straight lines. Leys can also be indicated by early Christian sites, at medieval churches, chapels and crosses from before the Reformation. This is because the Pope, in 601 A.D., ordered that pagan sites be used for Christian purposes. Not all the churches listed in these appendices have been confirmed as ancient. In an area heavily occupied over 6,000 years, some alignments may occur by chance, others may be lost due to agriculture or building developments over the same period.

Leys probably originated as Neolithic farming calendars, since the latter are essential for agriculture: when to plough, sow, harrow and harvest and when to prepare for winter, to kill and preserve the meat from animals not able to be fed. Neolithic monuments include long barrows, some round barrows, megaliths, stone circles (which are rarely circular), henges, observatories and settlement sites. Such features were often back sights for observing astronomical events like dawn occurring at horizons, hence the use of prominent hills, slopes and cols (horizon niches) as fore sights. In some cases caves, lakes and fords occur on leys.

Ley alignments are invariably straight, like sunbeams. The sun was seen as a god, vital for the fertility of crops and animals. Hence, no doubt, religious rituals developed at important sites for Neolithic farmers like the tombs (barrows) of their ancestors. These examples of considerable organised social effort were also a demonstration of land holding.

Straight lines on leys sometimes indicate sites which are not intervisible because markers, whether wood or stone, have been destroyed. Sometimes these have been broken up for roads or building stone, some have been dragged into hedges and some have been thrown down and buried. Some are still there if you can find them. Some stones marked on the 1880s Ordnance Survey 6" and 2½" maps, not recorded on modern maps, can still be found. In the appendices the use of the word 'site' (e.g. stone site) indicates that there was a stone but it may no longer be there.

When considering leys the angle of alignment can be a clue to its use, since from about 4000 B.C. the arrival of the first farmers used the rising and setting of the sun and moon and the major moon standstills as season and religious event markers. The reciprocal of angles should always be considered. Place names and folklore can also be clues to ley lines, as can the legends of early Christian saints. The latter, like dragons, can often have associations with wells.

The best way to check the validity of leys proposed in the appendices is to walk them and record what is there. Always observe the Countryside Code and obtain the landowners or occupiers consent. There will, no doubt, be examples of new information to be found and recorded. (It is important to share ideas.) Such data will include archaeological, topographical, historical, folklore, place name, religious and social considerations. Some proposed leys may then be disregarded and others reinforced. The destruction of much of prehistory leaves a lot to be detected.

# Appendix 1

**Hengistbury Head, southeast (now eroded)**

There are 13 possible ley lines which focus at the long groyne at the southeast end of the promontory which is Hengistbury Head. The groyne divides Christchurch Bay from Poole Bay, the entrance to the Western Solent. Hengistbury Head protects Christchurch Harbour, the route up the River Avon to Salisbury Plain and also the route up the River Stour which gave access to Cranborne Chase.

Salisbury Plain and Cranborne Chase were heavily utilised by the first farmers in the Neolithic period. The Head also gave views to and from the Isle of Wight and Purbeck.

The name Hengist can mean stallion; the horse was a totem animal to British Celts. The word bury means fort.

**H1**    Peveril Point, Isle of Purbeck (IOP) to Great Ballard Lake,  New Milton
      Length 26.5 kms     50° angle from Peveril point
      OS sheet 195

| | |
|---|---|
| 041 787 | Peveril Point (1½ miles south of Ballard Down, perhaps associated with Ballard Lake, New Milton) |
| 1775 9020 | Hengistbury Head eroded site at SE end |
| 243 957 | Stone site at the north side of Great Ballard Lake, New Milton |

**H2**    Worth Matravers Church IOP to Furzey Lodge, New Forest
      Length 46 kms     58° angle from Worth Matravers
      OS sheets 195/6

| | |
|---|---|
| 072 775 | Worth Matravers Church |
| - | Godlingstone (possible stone name/site) |
| - | Ballard Down (perhaps derived from Baal, a Phoenician god*) |
| 0461 8202 | King Barrow |
| 055 825 | Handfast Point (ley node) |
| 055 825 | Old Harry's Wife (rock in sea now fallen; Harry, a name for the devil) |

| | |
|---|---|
| - | across Poole Bay |
| 1775 9020 | Hengistbury Head eroded site |
| - | Golden Hill, Hordle ('gold' a name found on leys) |
| 324 993 | Boldre Church (possible pagan site) |
| 3645 0193 | Barrow near Furzey Lodge, New Forest |

\* Phoenician traders came into the English Channel from Cadiz after 800 B.C. and visited Hengistbury

**H3**   Swyre Head IOP to Fawley Church, New Forest to Warsash
Length 61.2 kms      64° angle from Swyre Head
OS sheets 195/6

| | |
|---|---|
| 934 785 | Swyre Head (trig point on hill top) |
| 9555 7955 | Kingston Church |
| 995 815 | Woolgarston Long Barrow (Neolithic ossury) possible stone name |
| 9965 8205 | Barrow at Kingswood |
| 0231 8285 | Agglestone (a logan stone\*) |
| - | across Studland and Poole Bay |
| 1775 9020 | Hengistbury Head eroded site |
| - | Hoopers Hill |
| - | Buckland Rings Hill Fort, New Forset |
| 4745 0355 | Fawley Church, New Forest |
| - | River Hamble spit and entrance |
| 481 068 | Newton Church, east side of Southampton Water, south of Warsash |

\* A logan stone which once used to rock, the resulting pressure effect has electro-magnetic consequences on crystaline structures generating energy.

**H4**   Worbarrow Tout IOP to Exbury, New Forest
Length 58 kms      71° angle from Worbarrow Tout
OS sheets 194/5/6

| | |
|---|---|
| 868 795 | Worbarrow Tout (promontory), ('tout' is a lookout) |
| 911 801 | Steeple Church (site of a pre-church cross) |
| - | over Barneston (possible stone name) |
| 9409 8195 | Church Knowle Church (Knowle is a name associated with knoll, a rounded hill, and is often found on leys) |

| | |
|---|---|
| 977 832 | Higher Bushey ley node |
| 986 836 | Bushey Barrow |
| - | across Poole Bay |
| 1775 9020 | Hengistbury Head, eroded site |
| - | across Christchurch Bay |
| - | across Lymington River |
| 4050 9725 | St Leonards's Chapel (a saint with a dragon association) |
| - | across River Ex |
| 4175 9865 | Exbury Hill Fort (promontory) |

**H5**  Drinking Barrow IOP to Two Sarsen Stones at the site of the former
Hordle Church

Length 36.1 kms        76° angle from Drinking Barrow
OS sheet 195

| | |
|---|---|
| 9112 8340 | Drinking Barrow |
| - | Sharford (Corfe River), a point crossed by three leys |
| - | Goathorn Peninsular |
| - | across Poole Harbour, north of Jerry's Point and south of South Haven Point |
| 1775 9020 | Hengistbury Head, eroded site |
| - | across Christchurch Bay |
| 2670 9265 | Two large fallen sarsen stones at site of old Hordle Church |

(the sarsen stones are possibly from Marlborough Downs in the Neolithic)

**H6**  Leigh Church, Blackmore Vale to Hill Top Barrow at western Isle of Wight
Length 73 kms        108° angle from Leigh Church
OS sheets 194/5/6

| | |
|---|---|
| 6175 0870 | Leigh Church (leigh is a ley name) |
| - | Ansty Cross |
| 866 005 | Barrow (most southerly of three) at East Down |
| - | Almer Church / Cross |
| - | Corfe Mullen (former Cross site) |
| 0677 9380 | Most southerly stone site (of two stones), stone SW of Talbot Village Church (modern church) |
| 1775 9020 | Hengistbury Head, eroded site |
| - | across Christchurch Bay and Western Solent |
| - | Hatherwood Point IOW |
| 315 857 | Barrow on hill at western end of Isle of Wight |

**H7**    Henbury, Sturminster Marshal to Hengistbury Head
Length 24.2 kms        109° angle from Henbury Barrow (possibly
                                                    approaching Imbolc/Samhain)

OS sheet 195
9478 9820    Henbury Barrow
0245 9564    a Canford Heath barrow
-            across Wallisdown (Wallis is Anglo-Saxon for foreigner
                                i.e the Britons and Welsh, hence Briton's Hill*)
0690 9400    Modern church at Talbot Village, situated between two
                                    stone sites SW and NE of the church
-            across Pokesdown (Puck's Hill). There were Bronze Age
                                barrows and Iron Age burials at Pokesdown
1775 9020    Hengistbury Head, eroded site

* About the time of Arthur, the British war leader 520 A.D., the Britons held Dorset and the Saxons held Christchurch (then called Tweoxneam – the place betwixt the waters) and Breamore in the Avon Valley (Hampshire).

**H8**    Long Barrow north of Blandford Camp to Hengistbury Head
Length 32 kms        127° angle from Long Barrow (Close to Winter
                            Solstice? Close to a Moon Standstill for Imbolc/Samhain?)

OS sheet 195
9225 0935    Long Barrow north of Blandford Camp
9293 0885    Long Barrow northeast of Blandford Camp
-            Merry Field Hill (dancing/rites?), north of Cole Hill
066 986      Longham Church (This is a modern, post-Reformation
                                    church.; random coincidence?)
076 979      Dudsbury Hill Fort, the line runs across the main entrance
                                    from River Stour.
             (Dud may derive from Dod, an ancient name for surveyor.)
153 921      Barrow at Wick
1585 9168    Stone site at Wick (stone shown on early OS maps but now
                                    gone)
1775 9020    Hengistbury Head, eroded site

**H9**    Woodcutts, Cranborne Chase to Hengistbury Head
      Length 35.8 kms     141° angle from Woodcutts (most southerly Moon
          Standstill for Imbolc/Samhain, reciprocal is most northerly Moon Set)
      OS sheets 184/195
      (same ley as Appendix 2, No.9)

|  |  |
|---|---|
| - | Settlement site at Woodcutts Common |
| - | Thorneydown |
| 995 140 | West end of Dorset Cursus |
| - | Harley Down |
| 0240 1025 | Knowlton ruined church in Neolithic henge |
| - | Knowle Hill (Knowle a name found on leys) |
| - | Wigbeth (beth means home of the god) |
| - | Summerlug Hill (lug - Lugh, a Celtic god) |
| - | Tricketts Cross (triple[?] – three is a Celtic sacred number) |
| - | East Parley Common close to a barrow |
| - | Blackwater (site of former ferry crossing, black is a ley name) |
| 1605 9245 | Christchurch Priory Church (built on Saxon Minster which was on a pagan site at the confluence of the rivers Avon and Stour, with dragon folklore) |
| 1775 9020 | Hengistbury Head, eroded site |

**H10**    Beacon Hill, Hindon to Hengistbury Head
      (same ley as St Catherine's Chapel see Appendix 3, No.4)
      Length 47.9 kms     145° angle from Beacon Hill
      OS sheets 184/195

|  |  |
|---|---|
| - | Beacon Hill |
| - | Old Wardour Castle (not known to be a prehistoric site) |
| - | Whitesheet Hill (white a name associated with leys) |
| - | Gallows Hill |
| - | Troy Down Barrow, 230m |
| - | Ackling Dyke (Roman Road) where it crosses Dorset Curcus |
| 0198 1472 | Long Barrow east of Down Farm south of Dorset Curcus |
| - | Rye Hill |
| - | Whitmore (whit – white, a name associated with leys) |
| 0915 0317 | Stone site at West Moors (central stone of five in the area) |
| - | Barrow at St Catherine's Hill |
| 1437 9523 | St Catherine's Chapel site |

|            | -         | east side of River Avon opposite Christchurch Castle Bailey |
| 1775 9020 | Hengistbury Head, eroded site |

**H11** Barrow at Plumbley Wood to Hengistbury Head
Length 20.9 kms   161° angle from Plumbley Wood Barrow
OS sheet 195

| 111 101 | Barrow at Plumbley Wood |
| 1115 0993 | Barrow at Plumbley Wood |
| - | Ashley |
| - | David's Hill |
| - | Leybrook Common (at least four ley names on this alignment) |
| 1375 0195 | most western of two stones sited east of River Avon at Bisterne |
| - | Avon Tyrell |
| - | close to west side of St Michael's Church, Sopley, east of River Avon |
| 1580 9615 | central stone of four sited at Ogber, west of Winkton (Og a name for sun. See St Catherine's ley Appendix 3, No. 1) |
| - | close west side of Tutton's Well (spring) |
| 1775 9020 | Hengistbury Head, eroded site |

**H12** Winterborne Stoke Settlement to Hengistbury Head
Length 52.8 kms   169° angle from Winterborne Stoke settlement
OS sheets 184/195

| - | Winterborne Stoke Settlement (close to Long Barrow) |
| - | Oatlands Hill |
| - | Druids Lodge |
| 3555 1024 | Newton Long Barrow |
| - | Fugglestone |
| - | Castle Ditches Hill Fort (tangent to east side) |
| - | Whitbury (whit a name found on leys) |
| 1450 1015 | Harbridge Church, west of River Avon |
| 1720 9379 | Staple Cross (on top of a mound before by-pass built) |
| 1775 9020 | Hengistbury Head, eroded site |

**H13** Ludgershall to Hengistbury Head

Length 61.5 kms       188° angle from Ludgershall towards the sun at its
zenith

OS sheets 184/195

| | |
|---|---|
| 263 512 | Ludgershall Norman Castle (possibly on Iron Age or earlier site) |
| 263 509 | Ludgershall Church (Lugh, Celtic god) |
| - | Snoddington Down (possible 'Dod' word associated with surveyors and alignments) |
| - | Cholderton Hill (possible 'cold' or 'cole' word found on leys) |
| - | Boar Hill (boar a beast of heraldic significance to the Celts) |
| 250 397 | Martin's Clump earthwork (clump, tump, tout words associated with leylines and lookouts) |
| 247 374 | Isle of Wight Hill (long range view point) |
| 242 336 | highest point (trig point) at East Winterslow |
| - | across col between Dean Hill and Pepperbox Hill |
| 215 157 | Barrow southwest of Studley Castle |
| 2105 1250 | Earthwork at Holly Hatch |
| - | Handy Cross Plain |
| - | Ridley Plain |
| 1983 0385 | Burley Hill Fort (dragon folklore) |
| - | Black Bush (black, a name found on leys) |
| 1967 0282 | Barrow at Burley Beacon (dragon folklore) |
| - | Dur Hill Down (½km west of Lugden Barrow) |
| - | Lob's Hole (fresh water spring in Christchurch Harbour, named for Celtic god Lugh) |
| 1775 9020 | Hengistbury Head, eroded site |

# Appendix 2

**Christchurch Priory Church (has dragon folklore, carvings and paintings)**
Possible ley lines which pass through the Priory Church of the Holy Trinity on a pagan site. Trinity may be a reminder of the triple number sacred to pagan Celts.

**P1**    Wick to Golden Cross
Length 26.1 kms        12° angle from the stone site at Wick, reciprocal 192°
OS sheets 184/195

| | |
|---|---|
| 1585 9170 | Stone site at Wick |
| 1605 9245 | Christchurch Priory Church |
| 1690 9680 | suspected Long Barrow site (destroyed) at North Bockhampton |
| - | Crow Hill (crow, black bird like a raven, associated with leys) |
| - | Knaves Ash |
| - | Picket Post? |
| - | Marrowbones Hill |
| 2065 1430 | Barrow at Amberwood Inclosure |
| - | Coopers Hill |
| - | Black Gutter Bottom (black a ley name) |
| - | Deadman's Hill (corpse roads were straight, like leys) |
| - | Jacob's Barrow (Jacob associated with ladder to Heaven in the Bible) |
| - | Golden Cross (gold a name associated with leys) |

**P2**    Durlston Down, Isle of Purbeck to Fox Hill, New Forest
Length 42.8 kms        45° angle from Durlston
OS sheets 195/6

| | |
|---|---|
| 0145 7760 | Durlston Down, 120m (east of trig point) a ley focus site |
| - | across Poole Bay east of Ballard Down |
| 1605 9245 | Christchurch Priory Church (Christchurch once called Edgegate – to the New Forest) |
| 1720 9379 | Staple Cross |
| - | Wilverley Plain (Wil a sun name, Ver an Earth Mother name, ley a clearing *) |

| | |
|---|---|
| - | Duck Hole |
| - | Foxlease (link to Fox Hill?) |
| - | Clayhill (Clay possible ley associated name) |
| - | White Moor (east of trig point). (White a ley associated name) |
| 315 085 | Fox Hill ley focus, also known as Bolton's Bench, a clump of trees |

\* The sun and Earth Mother unite at some Megalith sites e.g. Newgrange, Stonehenge.

**P3**   Godlingston Hill IOP to stone site north of Beckley, New Forest
Length 26.3 kms      54° angle from Godlingston Point
OS sheet 195

| | |
|---|---|
| 0086 8115 | Trig Point (199m) Godlingston Hill (possible stone site) |
| - | Dean Hill |
| - | across Studland and Poole Bays |
| 1605 9245 | Christchurch Priory Church |
| 2192 9700 | Stone site north of Beckley, east of East Close Hotel |
| | (a Saxon Hundred Moot may have met in this area) |

**P4**   Puckstone Isle of Purbeck to Wootton Stone, New Forest
Length 26.8 kms      56° angle from Puckstone
OS sheet 194/5

| | |
|---|---|
| 0121 8312 | Puckstone |
| - | across Poole Bay |
| 1530 9210 | Wick Barrow |
| 1605 9245 | Christchurch Priory Church |
| - | NW of Cat and Fiddle, Hinton |
| 2442 9830 | Wootton Stone, Sarsen Stone at old parish boundary between Milton and Brockenhurst |
| - | line continues close to trig point on Yew Tree Heath (not included in the length) |

**P5**   Dungy Head, Isle of Purbeck to Great Ballard, New Forest
Length 45.2 kms      70° angle from Dungy Head
OS sheets 194/5

| | |
|---|---|
| - | Dungy Head (edge of small promontory) |

| | |
|---|---|
| 8655 8185 | most northerly barrow at Ferny Barrow, East Lulworth |
| - | Whiteway (ley word) |
| - | north of Creech Barrow |
| 9215 8388 | Icen Barrow |
| - | Creech Heath (ley word) |
| 938 844 | close to north of Three Barrows |
| - | Wytch Peninsular (witch folklore found on some leys) |
| - | across Poole Harbour and Furzey Island |
| 0284 8775 | Brownsea Island Church |
| - | Flag Head Chine |
| - | across Poole Bay |
| 1433 9195 | Stone site at Southbourne |
| 1605 9245 | Christchurch Priory Church |
| - | Purewell Cross (roads) |
| - | Hoborne Hill (now Saulflands). (Hob a by-name for the Celtic god Lugh) |
| 2425 9560 | Stone site on west side of Great Ballard Lake, New Milton |

**P6** Stone site at Parkstone to Two Sarsens at the former Hordle Church site
Length 23.4 kms  90° angle from Parkstone (Equinox)
OS sheet 195

| | |
|---|---|
| 0328 9232 | Stone site at Parkstone on hill |
| - | south of Fern Barrow |
| - | Pokesdown (hill top named for Puck, the Nature god) |
| 1605 9245 | Christchurch Priory Church |
| 1715 9250 | Tutton's Well (spring) |
| - | across Christchurch Bay south of Friars Cliff barrow |
| 2670 9265 | Two large fallen sarsen stones at site of the former Hordle Church |

(sarsen stones probably taken in Neolithic from Marlborough Downs)

**P7** Tarrant Keyneston Church to Christchurch Priory Church
Length 26.1 kms  117° angle from Wimborne
OS sheet 195

| | |
|---|---|
| 9245 0405 | Tarrant Keyneston Church |
| - | south of Straw Barrow |
| - | south of Badbury Rings Hill Fort |

| | |
|---|---|
| 0090 9995 | Wimborne Minster, church on a Roman site |
| 0317 9880 | Canford Church |
| - | Red Hill (red associated with leys) |
| 1155 9465 | Holdenhurst Long Barrow |
| - | across Iford on east side of River Stour |
| 1605 9245 | Christchurch Priory Church |

**P8**  Iwerne Minster to Lob's Hole, Christchurch Harbour
Length 38.8 kms      127° angle from Iwerne Minster
OS sheets 194/5

| | |
|---|---|
| 868 145 | Iwerne Minster (church) |
| - | Grammars Hill (perhaps once Grandma's Hill i.e. the Old Mother – Earth Mother's Hill) |
| - | Gunville Down |
| 9440 0880 | Tarrant Monkton Church |
| - | Dean Hill (ecclesiastical name) |
| - | Cannon Hill (ecclesiastical name) |
| - | Parley Green |
| - | through barrow site near Fitzmaurice Road, Jumpers |
| 1605 9245 | Christchurch Priory Church |
| 1795 9108 | Lob's Hole, freshwater spring in Christchurch Harbour (Lob, Celtic god Lugh) |

**P9**  Woodcutts, Cranborne Chase to Hengistbury Head, eroded site
Length 35.8 kms      141° angle from Woodcutts (most southerly Moon
   Standstill for Imbolc/Samhain, reciprocal 321° is most northerly Moon Set)
OS sheets 184/195
Same ley as Hengistbury Head, Appendix 1, No. 9

| | |
|---|---|
| - | Settlement site at Woodcutts Common |
| 995 140 | West end of Dorset Cursus |
| - | Harley Down |
| 0240 1025 | Knowlton ruined church in Neolithic henge |
| - | Knowle Hill (knowle a word found on leys) |
| - | Wigbeth (beth means home of the god) |
| - | Summerlug Hill (lug - Lugh, a Celtic god) |
| - | Tricketts Cross (triple[?] – three is a Celtic sacred number) |
| - | East Parley Common close to a barrow |

| | |
|---|---|
| - | Blackwater (site of former ferry crossing, black is a ley name) |
| 1605 9245 | Christchurch Priory Church |
| 1775 9020 | Hengistbury Head, eroded site |

**P10** Settlement at Cow Down, south of Warminster, to Christchurch Priory
Length 51.7 kms          150° angle from a point at Cow Down
OS sheets 184/195
(same ley as St Catherine's, Appendix 3, No. 5)

| | |
|---|---|
| - | Settlement site at Cow Down (Warminster known for many UFO reports) |
| - | Starveall (possibly Star Fall, a phrase which links to astronomy) |
| - | Stonehill (possible megalith site) |
| - | Cold Berwick Hill (cold/cole associated with leys) |
| - | Swallowcliffe Down |
| - | Middle Down |
| - | northeast of Alvediston Church (possibly over original cross or church site) |
| - | South Down Stonedown 220m (possible megalith site) |
| - | Barrow Cemetery at Oakley Down, NE edge of most western barrow |
| 0182 1710 | Barrow north side of Akling Dyke |
| - | Dorset Cursus, longest Neolithic earthwork in NW Europe |
| - | Creech Hill (creech name possibly associated with leys) |
| - | NW side of Barrow at Woodland Common |
| - | Barrow at Redman's Hill (red a name associated with leys) |
| - | Barrow and earthworks SE of Redman's Hill |
| - | Stone site at NE side of West Moors Plantation |
| - | Barrow at Ramsdown |
| - | Barrow at St Catherine's Hill |
| 1437 9523 | St Catherine's Chapel site |
| 1605 9245 | Christchurch Priory Church, shares moving stones folklore with the Chapel site |

**P11** Harnham Church, Salisbury to Christchurch Priory Church
Length 36.9 kms          177° angle from Harnham Church, close to zenith of
sun

OS sheets 184/195

| | |
|---|---|
| - | possible Long Barrow at Larkhill } |
| - | The Avenue at Stonehenger } not included in length |
| - | East side of Normanton Down } estimate |
| - | East side of Old Sarum Hill Fort } |
| 1388 2930 | Harnham Church (Salisbury used a dragon in street theatre) |
| - | East side of Odstock Down |
| - | New Court Down |
| 1450 1380 | Fordingbridge Church |
| - | Ibsley |
| - | Blashford |
| - | Ringwood |
| - | Bisterne (dragon folklore) |
| 1565 9670 | St Michael's Church, Sopley (Michael a dragon killer) |
| 1575 9595 | most southerly stone (of four) at Ogber, west of River Avon (Og a name associated with Celtic god Lugh) |
| 1605 9245 | Christchurch Priory Church |

**P12**   Stone site at Bisterne to Christchurch Priory Church
Length 8.9 kms        179° angle from Bisterne, almost zenith of sun
OS sheet 195

| | |
|---|---|
| 1574 1042 | Stone site at Bisterne (dragon folklore) |
| 1588 9630 | Stone, most northerly (of four) at Ogber west of River Avon (Og name associated with Celtic god Lugh) |
| 1605 9245 | Christchurch Priory Church |

There may possibly be a 13th alignment to Christchurch Priory Church site from a Long Barrow at Queen's Bower, a hunting lodge site in the New Forest, NW of Boldreford, SE of Poundhill Heath; via a Barrow at Ober Heath east of Rhinefield and thence over Wilverly Plain (Wil a sun name, Ver an Earth Mother name). This is recorded as a ley on the summary at Appendix 4, but is not shown on the map of leys for the focus points of Appendices 1-3.

# Appendix 3

(Information from *St Catherine's Hill, a short history* published by Natula Publications 2005)

## St Catherine's Hill Chapel site, St Catherine's Hill

**C1**   Ridgeway Hill, Isle of Purbeck to Barrow at Matley Heath, New Forest
Length 48.8 kms       59° angle, approaching Beltaine/Lammas Sunrise
and Imbolc/Samhain Moon Rise

OS sheets 195/6

| | |
|---|---|
| 9185 9180 | high point (200m) Ridgeway Hill |
| - | close to NW side of barrow on Stonehill Down (perhaps once site of megalith) |
| - | across Corfe River south of Sharford Bridge (perhaps once site of a ford) a point crossed by three leys |
| - | Wytch Farm (witch folklore can be associated with leys) |
| - | northern tip of Green Island |
| - | eastern end of Furzey Island |
| - | stone at Brownsea Island (possibly modern) |
| - | north of Westbourne Church (modern hence no ley significance) |
| - | north of stone site at Queen's Park |
| 1437 9523 | St Catherine's Chapel site (probably a pagan site, inside a Roman signal station fort*) |
| 1580 9615 | Stone site at Ogber (sun fort) the most central of four west of River Avon (see Hengistbury Head Ley, Appendix 1, No. 11) |
| - | stone site at Ogber, most eastern of four |
| - | site of suspected Long Barrow at Clockhouse Farm, North Bockhampton (site destroyed by agriculture over 6,000 years and by Winkton Advanced Landing Ground used for Normandy Invasion 1944 ) |
| - | Bransgore crossroads, where ley line is one side of equilateral triangle (Bran, celtic god, name can mean raven; gore means triangle) |

|         |                                                              |
|---------|--------------------------------------------------------------|
| -       | Wilverley Plain (Wil a name for the sun, Ver a name for the  |
|         | Earth Mother)                                                |
| -       | Barrow on top of Holm Hill                                   |
| -       | Barrow north of Denny Wood                                   |
| 3405 0693 | Barrow at Matley Heath                                     |

\* The chapel existed by 1300 (probably before that time since rebuilt or repaired several times). Excavation produced a limestone slab (not local stone) painted with a fish, an early Christian symbol. The hill's name locally called Katterns, indicates pre-Christian activity related to the Earth Mother in her third form as Crone (bringer of death required in fertility cycle for new life). The pagan name was probably Kat Ann (Kali in Hindu, a religion with many similarities to that of Celts).

**C2**   Lodge Hill Barrow, Canford Heath to Golden Hill, Hordle
Length 23.6 kms        90° angle from Lodge Hill (Equinox)
OS sheet 195

| 0305 9525 | Lodge Hill Barrow |
|-----------|-------------------|
| -         | north of present Holdenhurst Church, probably over site of original (Saxon) church, which in turn could have been a pre-Christian site |
| -         | across River Stour where the Domesday settlement of Bosley once stood on the east bank (bosig can mean a flash of light in Celtic), a possible supply point for the Roman Signal Station on St Catherine's Hill\* |
| 1437 9523 | St Catherine's Chapel site |
| -         | Barrow at western edge of Burton Common |
| -         | northern tip of a lake at Burton Common |
| -         | crossroads by Cat and Fiddle Inn |
| -         | Ashley (ley can mean a clearing, perhaps to permit an unobstructed view) |
| -         | Golden Hill (gold a word associated with leys |
| 2675 9525 | Hordle, a point where a footpath reaches the road from Downton to Hordle. |

The word Hordle may derive from Hoard Hill and indicate  the find of a coin hoard in Medieval times. Such hoards have been found in the area: Becton

Bunny, Holdenhurst, Hengistbury Head and could have been hidden in response to Saxon raids in Roman times or Viking raids in Saxon times.

* Bosley settlement was probably in use in 296 A.D. when the Roman Emperor had to order a reinvasion. A sea fog prevented the fleet from being reported as it entered the Western Solent. This reconquest indirectly lead to Constantine the Great becoming Emperor at York and years later he adopted Christianity as the official religion of the Empire. The difficulty in seeing under a sea fog may be why there were two repeating stations close to each other at Hordle and Milford.

**C3**  NE side Stourpaine Church, Cranborne Chase to St Catherine's Down, Isle of Wight.

Length 71.5 kms 116° angle from Stourpaine, close to Imbolc/Samhain dawn
OS sheets 194/5/6

| | |
|---|---|
| - | NE side Stourpaine Church, possibly site of earlier church or cross on pagan site |
| - | France Down |
| - | Long Barrow at Down Wood, NNW of Badbury Rings |
| - | between two Barrows at King Down |
| - | Colehill Church (cole a word associated with leys) |
| - | cross and recross River Stour at Merritown (merry a word associated with dancing and pagan rituals) |
| 1437 9523 | St Catherine's Chapel site, inside a Roman fort |
| - | site of stone NW of Staple Cross, once in a farmyard |
| 1720 9379 | Staple Cross, a damaged medieval cross once on top of a mound. Mound has disappeared due to changes in ground levels when by-pass built. |
| 1915 9287 | Barrow at Friars Cliff |
| - | across Christchurch Bay and Western Solent to Compton Bay, IOW |
| - | Hanover Point and Brook Bay, IOW |
| - | Barnes High, trig point on hill top, IOW |
| - | St Catherine's Down, IOW |

The name Catherine occurs on coastal hills often in sight of St Michael's Churches (as at Christchurch). Local Catherine Hills are at: Abbotsbury, Christchurch, Isle of Wight. All are likely to have been on Roman signal routes able via repeating stations to pass messages by fire or smoke (night or day) to the general at Porchester and the admiral at Bitterne. These Roman signal routes were probably based on pre-existing farming calendar sight lines. It is possible that St Aldhelm's Head at the Isle of Purbeck was once a Katterns Hill renamed for the Saxon saint.

The Romans had two signal towers attached to the fort on St Catherine's Hill. These could signal to East Hill at Corfe and via repeating stations to West Hill at Carisbrooke. These may have been on ley line alignments. Corfe could signal to Wareham and Carisbrooke to Porchester.

**C4**   Beacon Hill, Hindon to Hengistbury Head (same ley as Hengistbury, Appendix 1, No. 10)

Length 47.9 kms     145° angle from Beacon Hill
OS sheets 184/195

| | |
|---|---|
| - | Beacon Hill, 237m, south of Hindon, Wilts |
| - | Old Wardour Castle (not known to be a prehistoric site) |
| - | Whitesheet Hill (white a name associated with leys) |
| - | Gallows Hill |
| - | Troy Down Barrow, 230m |
| - | Ackling Dyke (Roman Road) where it crosses Dorset Cursus |
| 0198 1472 | Long Barrow east of Down Farm south of Dorset Cursus |
| - | Rye Hill |
| - | Whitmore (whit – white, a name associated with leys) |
| 0915 0317 | Stone site at West Moors (central stone of five in the area) |
| - | Barrow at St Catherine's Hill |
| 1437 9523 | St Catherine's Chapel site |
| - | east side of River Avon opposite Christchurch Castle Bailey |
| 1775 9020 | Hengistbury Head, eroded site |

**C5**   Settlement at Cow Down, south of Warminster to Christchurch Priory
                                                            Church

Length 51.7 kms     150° angle from a point at Cow Down
OS sheets 184/195
(same ley as Christchurch Priory Church, Appendix 2, No.10)

| | |
|---|---|
| - | Settlement site at Cow Down |
| - | Starveall (possibly Star Fall, a phrase which links to astronomy) |
| - | Stonehill (possible megalith site) |
| - | Cold Berwick Hill (cold/cole associated with leys) |
| - | Swallowcliffe Down |
| - | Middle Down |
| - | NE of Alvediston Church (possibly over original cross or church site) |
| - | South Down Stonedown 220m (possible megalith site) |
| - | Barrow Cemetery at Oakley Down, NE edge of most western barrow |
| 0182 1710 | Barrow north side of Akling Dyke |
| - | Dorset Cursus, longest Neolithic earthwork in NW Europe |
| - | Creech Hill (creech name possibly associated with leys) |
| - | NW side of Barrow at Woodland Common |
| - | Barrow at Redman's Hill (red a name associated with leys) |
| - | Barrow and earthworks SE of Redman's Hill |
| - | Stone site at NE side of West Moors Plantation |
| - | Barrow at Ramsdown |
| - | Barrow at St Catherine's Hill |
| 1437 9523 | St Catherine's Chapel site (shares moving stones folklore with the Priory Church) |
| 1605 9245 | Christchurch Priory Church (dragon folklore) |

**C6** Long Barrow east of Robin Hood's Ball, Wilts to St Catherine's Chapel site
Length 50.3 kms      176° angle approaching sun's zenith
OS sheets 184/195

| | |
|---|---|
| - | Long Barrow east of Robin Hood's Ball, NE of Rollestone Camp |
| - | between two Barrows at Fargo Plantation |
| - | Normanton Down (North man enclosure Hill) |
| - | Wilsford Down (Wil a name for the sun) |
| - | Lake Down |
| - | Boreland Hill |
| - | Earthworks north of Middle Woodford |

| | |
|---|---|
| - | Smithern Down |
| - | Camp Down |
| - | west of Bemerton Down |
| 1227 2601 | Homington Church |
| - | Castle Ditches Iron Age Hill Fort, tangent to west side |
| - | west of Whitsbury Church (Whit, name associated with leys) |
| - | Rockborne Roman Villa (possibly on an earlier site) |
| - | Black Hill (black a name associated with leys) |
| - | East of Somerley House (summer – sun at peak, ley – alignment) |
| - | Stone site most eastern of a pair east of Avon at Bisterne (dragon folklore) |
| - | Barrow on St Catherine's Hill |
| 1437 9523 | St Catherine's Hill Chapel site |

**C7** Frittleton Church, Wilts to Stone site at Southbourne
Length 67.4 kms      181° angle nearly due south, zenith of sun
OS sheets 184/195

| | |
|---|---|
| - | Frittleton Church |
| - | Netheravon Village |
| - | west of Woodhenge and Long Barrow |
| - | Amesbury Hill Fort |
| - | Amesbury Down |
| - | tangental to east side of Ogbury Hill Fort (Og a name of sun god) |
| - | west of High Post |
| - | Salterton Down |
| - | Church at Salisbury (east of cathedral) |
| - | east side of Odstock earthwork |
| - | New Court Down |
| - | Botley's Farm east of Gallows Hill |
| 1455 1383 | Fordingbridge Church |
| 1450 1015 | Harbridge Church |
| - | west of Ringwood Church (possibly original church site) |
| - | Barrow at St Catherine's Hill |
| 1437 9523 | St Catherine's Hill Chapel site |
| 1442 9200 | Stone site at Southbourne |

It is likely that those sites with the highest proportion of leys crossing them are the least due to coincidence. Hence besides those sites examined in Appendices 1-3 it would be useful to examine the suspected Long Barrow site at Clockhouse Farm, North Bockhampton, mentioned in the Christchurch Times in 1861, and the old Hordle Church site near the coast at Hordle Cliff. This demolished church, built in 1080 has two large fallen sarsen stones in its churchyard.

It is interesting to speculate if the four sites with 13 leys relate to the number of lunations in a solar year, the number in a coven and perhaps an early zodiac of 13 houses. Two of these four sites once held churches. Perhaps the lost chantry at Winkton was also at the Clockhouse site, rather than near Holfleet (Holy Stream).

It is likely that many calendar (Neolithic) alignments originated from the chalk hills of both Cranborne Chase and the Isle of Purbeck. Since the chalk was easier to work with stone tools and less overgrown than the wooded and flooded lower land. (See Appendix 4).

Further information would be welcome concerning any antiquities or folklore associated with ley crossing sites or alignments, including the original dedications for churches and chapels on leys, since some saints have dragon legends, as would any local dragon folklore. Please contact Michael A. Hodges in writing c/o Natula Publications, 5 St Margarets Avenue, Christchurch, Dorset BH23 1JD

# Appendix 4
## Sketch of ley focus sites at Christchurch indicating the coastline at Hengistbury before the effect of 19th and 20th century erosion

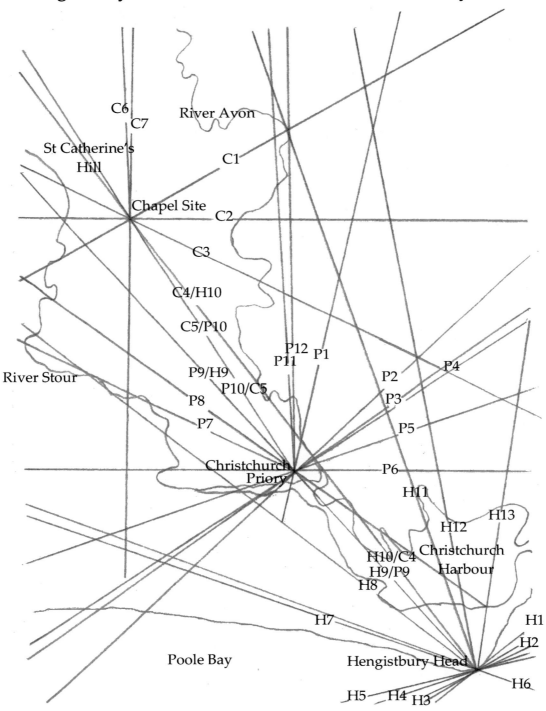

# Some multiple Ley Focus Sites in, or visible from, the Christchurch Area

The same alignment may go through several sites

| No. of leys crossing site | Hengistbury App.1 | Priory App.2 | Chapel App.3 | Location |
|---|---|---|---|---|
| 13 | 13 | | | Hengistbury Head eroded site |
| 13 | 1 | 1 | 1 | Suspected Long Barrow, North Bockhampton |
| 13 | 1 | 1 | 1 | Hordle old church site, 2 sarsen stones |
| 13 | | 13 | | Christchurch Priory Church |
| 7 | | | 7 | St Catherine's Hill, chapel site |
| 7 | 1 | | | Lob's Hole, Chewton Bunny, eroded |
| 7 | | 1 | | Stone site, Bisterne Farm |
| 6 | 1 | | | Stone site west side of Great Ballard Lake |
| 6 | | 1 | | Stone site north of Beckley |
| 6 | | | | Stone site near Lymington Road/Station Road, New Milton |
| 6 | 1 | 1 | 1 | Staple Cross, Burton |
| 5 | 1 | 1 | | Holdenhurst Long Barrow Site |
| 5 | 1 | 1 | | Stone site at Wick |
| 5 | | | | Most southern (of two) stone sites, West Southbourne |
| 5 | | | | Fallen sarsen stone, Westover, Milford-on-Sea |
| 5 | | 1 | | Sarsen stone at Wootton |
| 5 | | | | Stone site, Lugden Barrow, Dur Hill |
| 4 | | | | Lob's Hole, spring in Christchurch Harbour |

| | | | |
|---|---|---|---|
| 4 | 1 | 1 | Stone site at Southbourne |
| 4 | 1 | | West (of two) stone sites, Bisterne |
| 4 | 1 | | Tutton's Well |
| 4 | | | The Needles, Isle of Wight |
| 4 | 1 | 1 | Peveril Point, Isle of Purbeck |
| 3 | 1 | 1 | Wick Barrow |
| 3 | | 1 | Friars Cliff Barrow |
| 3 | | 1 | Stone site NW of Staple Cross |
| 3 | 1 | 1 | Central stone site (of four) at Ogber |
| 3 | 1 | | Northern stone site (of four) at Ogber |
| 3 | 1 | 1 | St Michael's Church, Sopley |
| 3 | | 1 | Milford on Sea Church |
| 3 | 1 | 1 | Stone site north side of Great Ballard Lake |
| 3 | | | Stone site, Manor Farm, Ossemsley |
| 3 | | | Old Harry Rocks, Isle of Purbeck |
| 2 | 1 | | Old Harry's Wife (fallen), Isle of Purbeck |
| 2 | 1 | 1 | SW stone (of four), Ogber |
| 2 | | 1 | Eastern stone (of four), Ogber |
| 2 | | 1 | Eastern stone (of two), Bisterne |
| 2 | | | Northern stone site (of two), West Southbourne |
| 2 | 1 | | Queen's Park stone site |
| 2 | | | Old Milton Church |

There are known to be very many alignments in the British Isles and hence far more ley focus sites outside the area of those shown above. There are possibly still more to be found for some of the above sites.

# Appendix 5

## Sketch to show sun calendar, observer in centre, horizon at edge

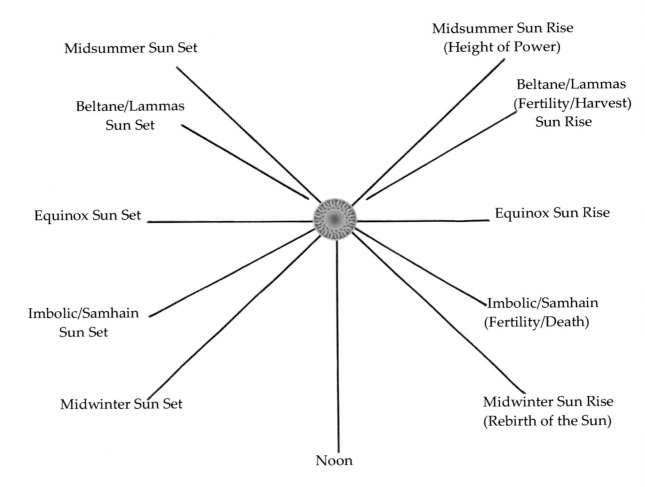

A moon calendar was no doubt also used employing major standstills. Time was counted in moons. Each day started at dusk, hence the eve (evening) was when celebrations began e.g. May Eve (30th April). Folklore frequently refers to activities at different states of the moon – waxing or waning; new moons were often mentioned. The moon may also have been used to help predict tides, important for coastal travel; also eclipses, important for religious purposes.

# Appendix 6

## Names Associated with Leys

Aggle (a stone that rocks)

Ann, Anne, Anu (god or goddess, chief of the Shining Ones [first farmers])

Ark (see Quoit) a place of mystery, power, weapon, transceiver

Arrow, Beam, Bolt, Shaft (weapon or ray of sun)

Ball (hill shape, see Knowle)

Beacon (see Fire, Taine, Trendle, Burnt)

Beans (folklore says sleep in a beanfield risks losing soul or gain knowledge)

Bel (Bell, Bil, Bill, Will, William, Wivel, Wyfel, Lian, Liam, Og, Ugh, Sil, Sal, Sol,
Sul – names for sun?)

Bell (see Bel)

Bemp

Bethel (see El, beth is 'home of' in Hebrew)

Black, Blag (associated with death)

Bleak (see Black)

Bran (raven, god) associated with the male names Brian, Brendon

Bream (bright-beam)

Brendon (see Bran)

Bridget, Bride (goddess)

Bump (hill, see Clump, Tump)

Burgh, Bury, Bur, Ber (fort)

Burnt (see Fire, Beacon)

But, Butts (place where shafts appear)

Caer (see Cairn)

Cairn (pile of stones)

Clump (see Tump)

Col, Cole (can be personal name or black or charcoal or hazel)

Cold (may relate to Col)

Corth (see Quorth)

Creech

Cross (can be a rtiual site)

Crow (as the crow flies – straight line)

Crystal (see Glass, could be used to generate fire from sunbeams)

Cursus (possible processional way)

Dance (see Whirl)

Death Road (always straight)

Devil, Devil's Seat, Devil's Quoits, Devil's Bed and Bolster etc

Dod, Dodd, Dodder, Dodding (name of Dodman – surveyor with two sighting
poles)

Dragon, Orm, Worm, Serpent

Edmund (royal saint martyred by arrow)

El (god)

Ely

Fair Lady (goddess)

Fairy

Fi (see Phi)

Fiddler (see Piper)

Fire (see Beacon)

Five (followed by Crosses, Lanes, Ways etc) five points to Star of Venus (five
cycles of 8 years i.e. 40 years)

George (Saint who tended to be adopted in place of Michael after Crusades,
could also be the Green Man)

Ghost (often reported on leys)

Glass (see Crystal)

Glaston, Glastonbury (glass enclosure fort, glass made there? Possibly due to
fire creating lens, the Grail?)

Goblin (see Devil – Hobgoblin)

Gold, Golden (associated with sun)

Grange (church farm)

Green George (see George)

Green Man (see George)

Grim (see Devil)

Hail, Hayel (can derive from Celtic word for sun)

Hel, Hele, Hell, Helis (see Hail)

Hob, Hod, Hobby Horse (see Lugh)

Holy, Holly (Holy Trinity)

Hor (dirty – muddy)

Howe

Hurl, Hurle, Throw

Hythe

Knoll, Know, Knowle (rounded hill, knowledge?)

Lady (goddess)

Lea, Lee, Leigh, Ley (word end or beginning), Leye, Ly, Lye (Ly at word end
can mean clearing)

Leape, Lip, Lipp, Lyp, Lymp

Lease

Liam (see William)

Lob, Lud, Lug (see Lugh)

Lot (light)

Lugh aka Lew, Lir, Mercury, Hermes, Thoth, 'of the Silver Hand', 'of the
Shining Hand', The Shining One, Ugh, Ug, Ogmash, Shamash

Maiden (virgin and/or goddess)

Margaret (saint associated with dragons)

Mark (boundary stone)

May, Mai, Mae, Maien, Maes, Mary (fertility goddess)

May Pole (phallic symbol)

Merry (dancing place – sexual activity, see Whirl)

Michael (Mi Ka El) like unto God, archangel, leader of Heavenly Host. His
churches are often on pagan sites and on hill tops. The dragon was earth
energy tamed (not killed) by Michael – as  shown in the earliest church
sculptures.

Mump (Clump, Tump, lookout place)

Music (chanting, singing, drumming, dancing able to induce trance)

Observatory (astronomy)

Og (name for sun god, see Ugh)

Old – Devil, Old One, Old Man, Old Boy, Old Harry, Old Nick, Old Woman

Orm – Worm, Dragon, Serpent

Peas (see Beans)

Perro (ferro, ferra, fire)

Phi (see Fi – Fire)

Piper (see Fiddler)

Puck (fertility nature god)

Quoit (from Celtic Coetun, see Ark)

Quorth

Rad, Red, Rud, Rudder, Ruddy

Regil (royal)

Remp

Ring (as in circular dances)

Rol. Role, Roll (see Whirl)

Ruler – King (straight line, straight edge)

Sal, Sil (see Bel), Sol, Sun

Serpent (see Dragon)

Silver (associated with the moon)

Spirit

Spring (see Well)

Starve All (Star – star fall)

Stone, Stan, Staine, Ston (word endings)

Straight (dragons only fly in straight lines)

Taine (see Fire), Tan

Temple (place for ritual)

Three (Holy Trinity)

Throw (see Hurl)

Thurle (hole)

Tor (stone at high place)

Toot, Tot, Tout (lookout point, beacon site, watch tower)

Trendle (kindle – see Fire)

Tump (see Clump)

Ugh (see Lugh and Og)

Way (route)

Wedding (sex and dances)

Well (water) from underground

Whirl, Worle (turn around, dance in a circle, could be used to induce trance)

White, wit (often found on salt trade routes)

Wich, Witch

Wick, dairy farm, creek, settlement outside Roman fort

Wihelm, Will (see Bel)

William (protected one)

Wim, Whimble (fire axel – hard wood spun in soft wood to make fire by friction)

Wivel (see Bel)

Worm (see Orm)

Wyfel (see Bel)

# About the Author

Michael A. Hodges, MA, FCIPD, MCMI, has taken part in many local history organisations. He has been Chairman of: The Christchurch Local History Society, The Friends of the Red House Museum, The Society of Ley Hunters, The Dorset Earth Mysteries Group and is active in The Dorset History Forum and The Dorset Archaelogical Committee. He is also a former Mayor of the Borough of Christchurch.

Besides writing a range of magazine articles, he is also an author of local history books:

Prepared for Battle, a military history of the Christchurch Area, 1982
Churchill (Somerset) a brief history of the Civil Parish, 1994 revised 1996
Churchill Parish and World War II, 1996
Helis the Cerne Giant and links with Christchurch, 1998
The Smuggler No Gentleman, smuggling with violence around Christchurch and Poole Bays, 1999, *Natula Publications*
Christchurch in World War II, parts 1 and 2, 2001, *CLHS*
Christchurch, a Photographic History, 2001 *Black Horse Books*
Christchurch Occasional Papers, 2001, *CLHS* for Town Centre Forum
Ghosts of Christchurch Hundred, 2002, *Natula Publications*
Christchurch Castle, 2003, *Natula Publications*
Christchurch the Golden Years, 2003, *Halsgrove*
Knowlton Rings, 2004, *Society of Ley Hunters*
Christchurch Town and City Memories, 2005, *Frith Books*
St Catherines Hill (Christchurch), a short history, 2005, *Natula Publications*

Michael takes guided walks for Christchurch Borough Council's Information Centre and gives lectures on local history topics.